Canadian Rockies Photo Album

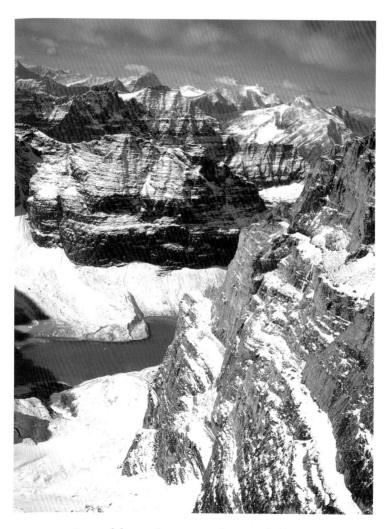

Gem-like Lake Oesa, beautifully set
in a snow-white border, as seen from Abbott Pass
in Yoho National Park.

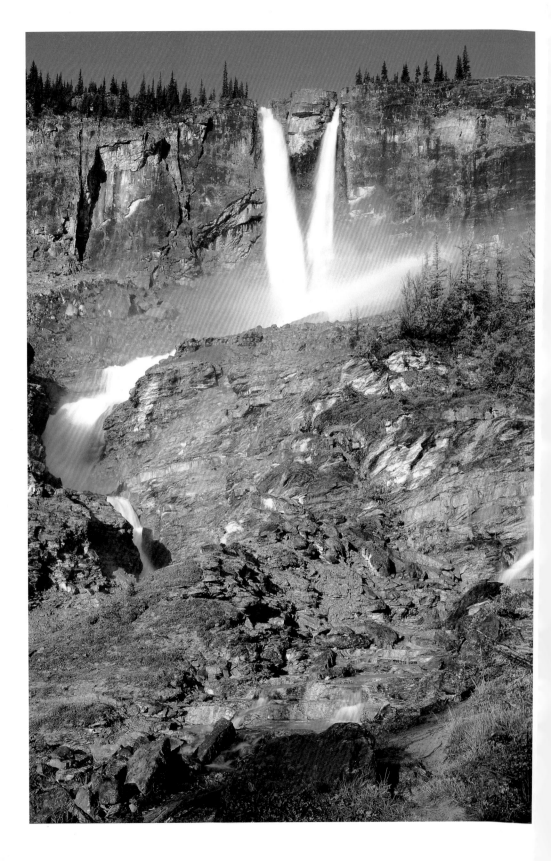

Canadian Rockies
Photo Album

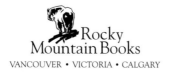
Rocky
Mountain Books
VANCOUVER • VICTORIA • CALGARY

Rocky Mountain Books
#108 – 17665 66A Avenue
Surrey, BC V3S 2A7
www.rmbooks.com

Rocky Mountain Books
PO Box 468
Custer, WA
98240-0468

Library and Archives Canada Cataloguing in Publication

Wilson, Elizabeth, 1961-
Canadian Rockies photo album / Elizabeth Wilson. — 1st Rocky
Mountain Books ed.

ISBN 978-1-897522-23-3

1. Rocky Mountains, Canadian (B.C. and Alta.)—Pictorial works.
I. Title.

FC219.W585 2009   971.10022'2
C2008-907326-6

Library of Congress Control Number: 2009920191

Photo overleaf: A rainbow born of water and sun descends into the
mist of Twin Falls in Yoho National Park.

Printed in Canada

Rocky Mountain Books acknowledges the financial support for its
publishing program from the Government of Canada through the
Book Publishing Industry Development Program (BPIDP), Canada
Council for the Arts, and the province of British Columbia through
the British Columbia Arts Council and the Book Publishing Tax Credit.

Contents

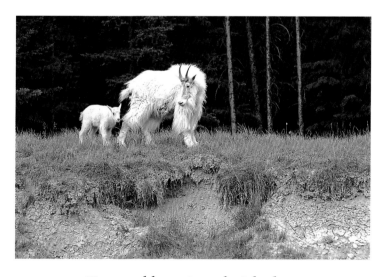

Tempted by mineral-rich clay,
a mountain goat and her kid have descended
from the mountainside for the day.

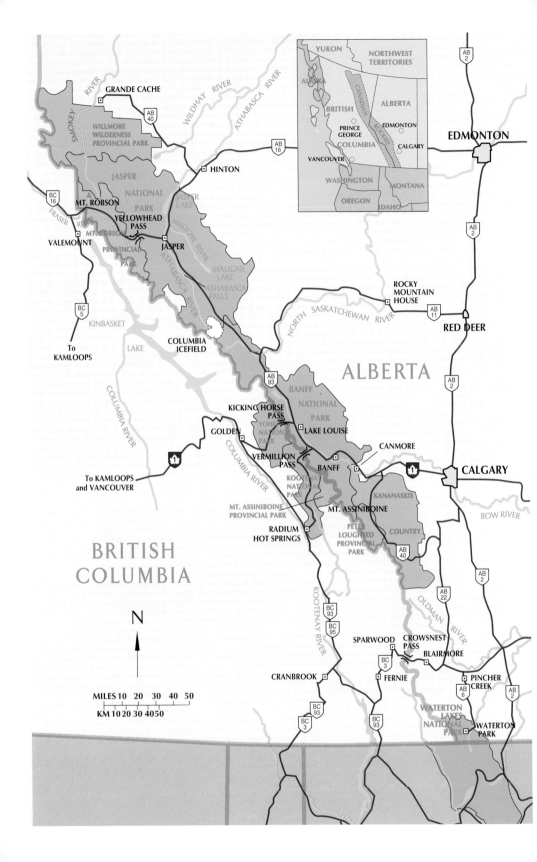

Welcome to the Canadian Rockies

People have been photographing the miracle of the Canadian Rocky Mountains for over 100 years, and they've probably had as many different reasons for doing so as there are reasons for coming here.

Over 11,000 years ago, Native people traveled, hunted and lived here. The fur traders came next, in the mid-1700's, followed by a handful of scientists, adventurers, missionaries and explorers. The construction of the Canadian Pacific Railway in the 1880's opened the area to the world once and for all, and the formation of the mountain parks preserved it.

These days people come to the Canadian Rockies to see the famous aquamarine waters of the mountain lakes, or for a chance to see a bear or a moose in its natural habitat. Some come for the birdwatching, or because they believe in the healing properties of mineral hot springs, or because they've always wanted to see a blue glacier. Perhaps most often, people come for the mountains themselves – to climb them, hike them, ski them, photograph them. To see them.

The *Canadian Rockies Photo Album* is a collection of nearly 150 extraordinary photographs. We hope these memorable images will help to make the Rockies unforgettable for you.

Waterton Lakes

When compared to the fleeting length of human existence, mountains seem to last forever.

As elsewhere in the Rockies, nomadic Natives were the first inhabitants in the lovely Waterton Lakes region. With the retreat of glacial ice 11,000 years ago, they began to hunt and fish in the valleys, following the migration of game between prairie and mountains.

Waterton is still a place where peaks meet prairie to stunning effect, because of the way mountain building happened here. Waterton became a national park in 1911 and, along with its neighbour Glacier National Park in Montana, was dedicated as an International Peace Park in 1932.

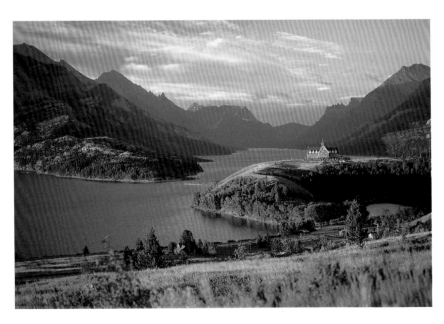

The Prince of Wales Hotel overlooks Waterton Lake, the deepest lake in the Canadian Rockies and one of the most beautiful.

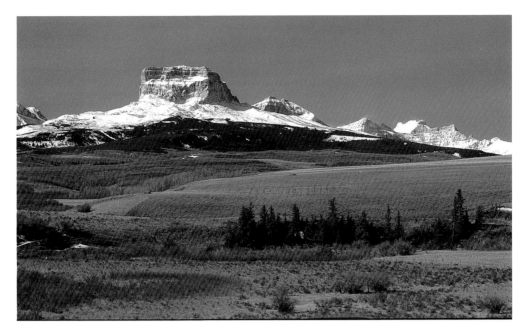

The aptly named Chief Mountain watches over
the plains that surround it.

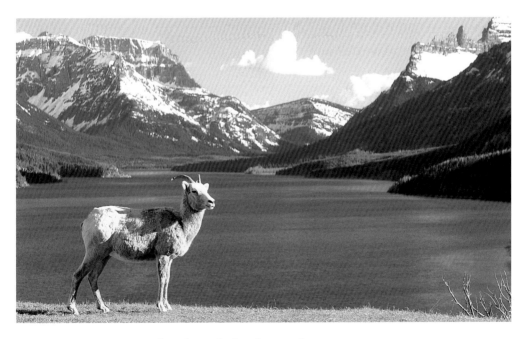

This female bighorn sheep is enjoying
a sunny day's grazing at Waterton.

Kananaskis and Assiniboine

This gorgeous 4000 sq km parcel of provincial land is tucked away to the south of the Trans-Canada Highway, just a tad off the beaten track, and despite the fact that the 1988 Winter Olympic Games were held here KANANASKIS COUNTRY is still visited less often than the national parks. Albertans know about the secret wonders of Kananaskis, though, and make good use of the area year-round.

Steeply tilted limestone peaks and valley bottoms rich with forest and grassland abound here, and the area is renowned for the variety of its wildlife. Provincial funds from the Alberta Heritage Savings Trust have been lavished on K-Country, and the opportunities for lovers of the outdoors are truly amazing. Hiking trails abound, as do campgrounds, bicycle paths, and lakes and streams for those who like fishing. The 36-hole Kananaskis Country golf course is one of the most spectacular in Canada.

Mt. Assiniboine's famous Matterhorn-shaped peak can be seen from high points in all directions in the tiny 386 sq km park that bears its name. MT. ASSINIBOINE PROVINCIAL PARK is rich in alpine meadows, larch trees and glacier-fed lakes and rivers, and as a result some of the finest hiking and wilderness skiing opportunities to be found anywhere in the Rockies are found right here. Assiniboine Lodge, one of the Rockies' premier backcountry lodges, nestles next to Lake Magog. This comfortable and charming establishmet offers a perfect base from which to explore the spectacular scenery of the Assiniboine Valley.

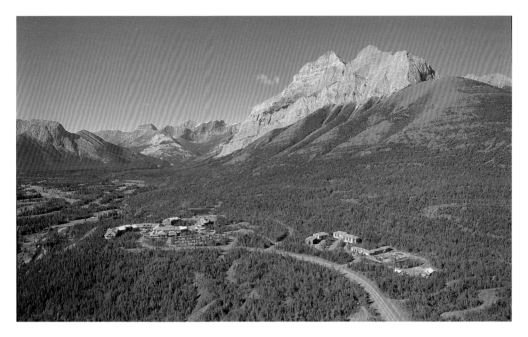

Kananaskis Village, with the famous Kananaskis golf course and Mt. Kidd in the background.

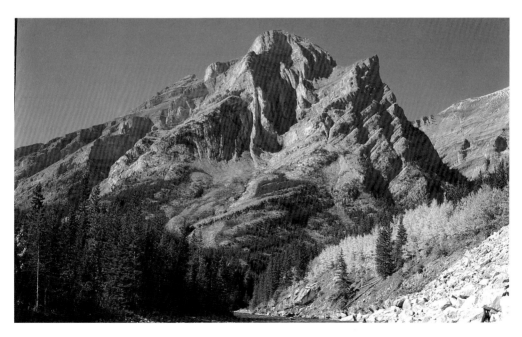

When the trees turn this vibrant yellow in the fall, Mt. Kidd's setting seems even more spectacular.

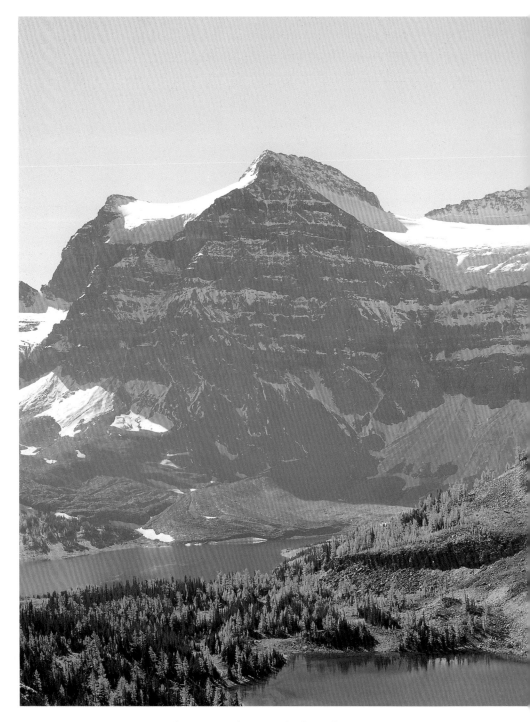

Mt. Assiniboine's glacier-clad peak contrasts
beautifully here with the calm, ice-blue waters of Sunburst Lake.

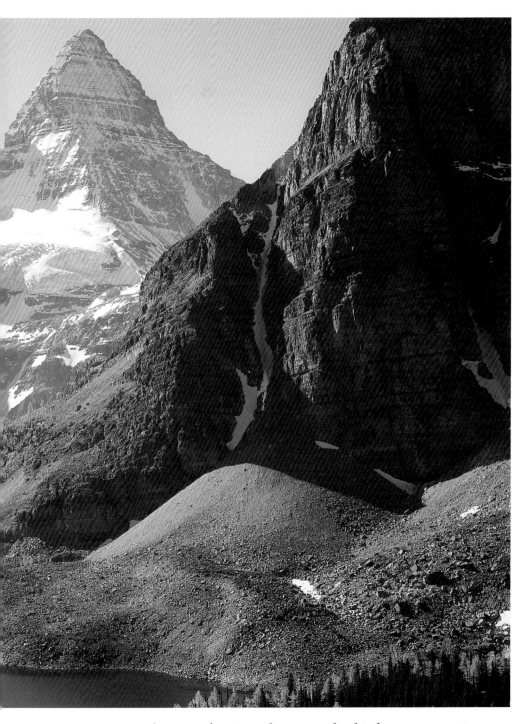

At 3618 m/11,870 ft, Assiniboine is the highest mountain
in the southern Canadian Rockies.

Banff

No matter how hard people try,
it's impossible to improve on what nature
put there in the first place.

Banff is the most famous of Canada's mountain parks, and there's always been something about it that inspires people to rhapsodize. In the 1930's, a brochure on Banff used the words of a prominent New York woman who visited:

I feel an irresistible urge to rave. There is sentimental music in the background and such a gorgeous view that I cannot keep my eyes on the paper. Anyone who wants to say 'See Naples and die' is welcome to do it. But this place makes me want to live to come back.

Canadians and visitors from around the world are incredibly lucky to find the well-preserved natural areas that Banff National Park protects, especially since the park's formation came about in such a strange and vaguely haphazard way.

In 1883, three Canadian Pacific Railway workers stumbled on what were to become known as the Cave and Basin Hot Springs and saw at once their promotional potential. However, dreams of fame and fortune quickly went up in the smoke of an ugly dispute that arose over ownership of the springs. To settle the matter, in 1885 the federal government stepped in to create Canada's first national park by setting aside 26 sq km of land around the springs as a federal reserve.

Once the track was laid, the CPR lost little time in building the Banff Springs Hotel in 1888 and then, at the turn of the century, Chateau Lake Louise. Wealthy and distinguished visitors swarmed to the new luxury resorts deep in the Canadian wilderness. When the first road between Banff and Lake Louise was opened in 1920, the entire valley was thrown open to an additional flood of visitors from across Canada, the United States and beyond.

In 1903 a visitor to Banff wrote:

The hot sulphur baths are wonderful: a deep pool in the rocks with the clearest of green sulphur water, quite warm – and oh! such a delightful sensation it gives you to bathe in it.

Banff's mineral hot springs are still a source of great pleasure to visitors, and new attractions and facilities are constantly being added for the year-round enjoyment of the six million plus people who come to one of the world's most popular tourist destinations annually.

But no matter how hard people try it's impossible to improve on what nature put there in the first place, and Banff National Park's magnificent wilderness is still its best feature by far.

Banff was Canada's first national park when it was created in 1885, and it was only the third national park to be created in the world (after Yellowstone in the United States and Royal in Australia). Today the park protects 6641 sq km/2563 sq mi of land and is part of the four mountain parks block. These parks were designated a World Heritage Site in 1984.

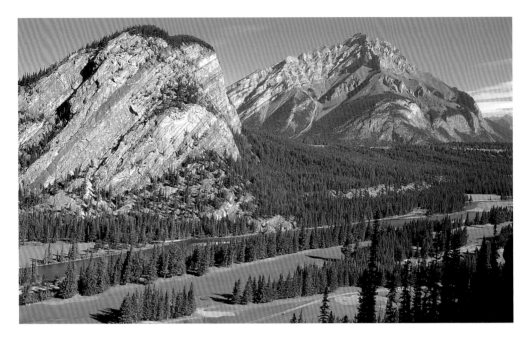

With surroundings like this, it's a wonder anyone can concentrate on the game when they play the world-class Banff Springs golf course.

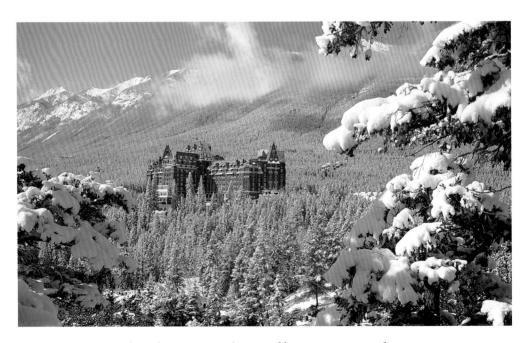

The chateau-style Banff Springs Hotel
is even more imposing in winter, with an army of
snow-clad trees surrounding it.

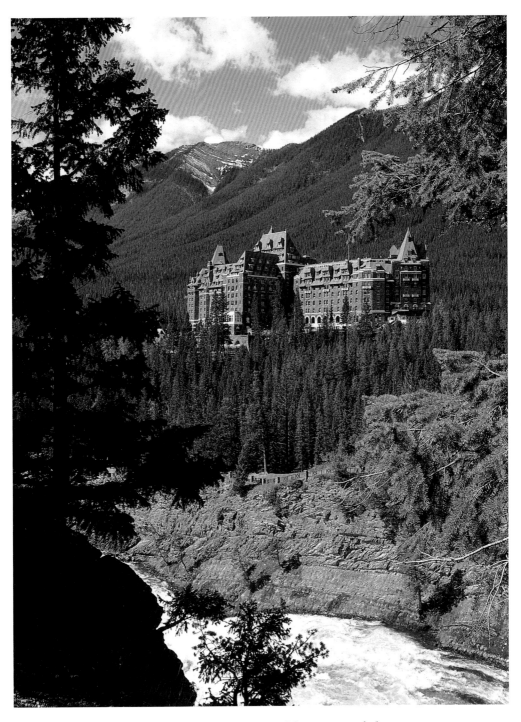

The Banff Springs Hotel has one of the most
spectacular settings in the world, surrounded by mountains
and overlooking the Bow River.

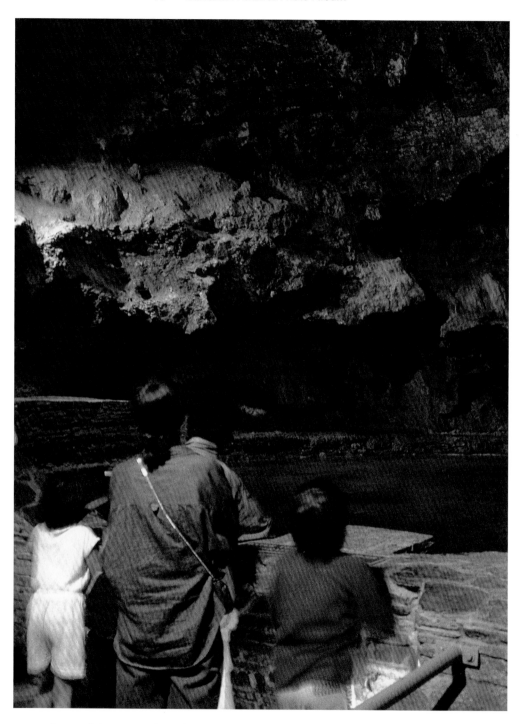

In the wild west a hot bath was a luxury, so the discovery of hot springs at the Cave and Basin was greeted with great enthusiasm.

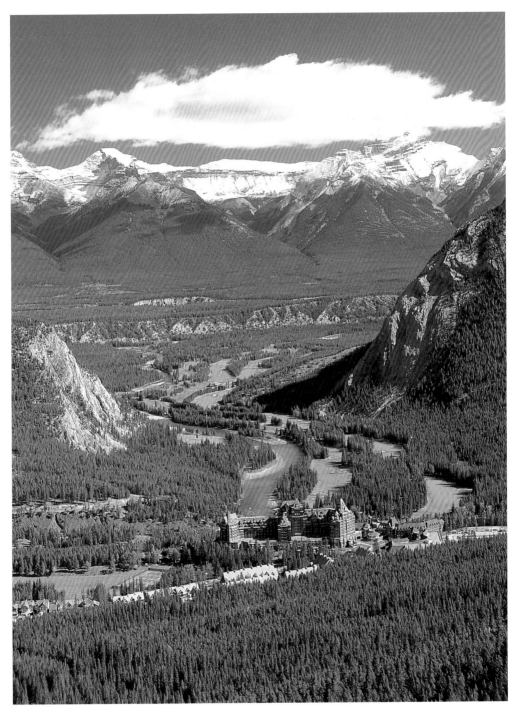

Banff Springs Hotel with the golf course
and the Fairholme Range in the Bow Valley.

On the Way
to the Wilderness

No matter which highway you take, the country between the towns of Banff and Lake Louise is very beautiful. The Trans-Canada Highway, which is the faster route, follows the south shore of the Bow River most of the way, while the Bow Valley Parkway, across the river, winds lazily uphill and downhill through thick evergreen forests. Many people take one route going, the other coming back, to get the best of both worlds.

In summer, the hiking trails along alpine meadows at Sunshine Village off the Trans-Canada are unsurpassed. The summit of the highest mountain in this part of the Rockies, Mt. Assiniboine, is visible from here, and the meadows themselves are delightful. The village offers excellent skiing in winter and a scenic gondola ride in summer so there's something for everyone.

On the other side of the Bow River, downstream from Lake Louise, Castle Mountain towers 2766 m/9076 ft above the valley floor like a mighty fortress. Castle is not all that high, but its formidable cliffs are very popular with rock and ice climbers.

A few miles to the east, along the Bow Valley Parkway, Johnston Canyon is accessible by footpath. A pleasant and gentle trail leads to the Lower and Upper Falls, which cascade between steep canyon walls. Cold water springs known as the Ink Pots lie in a peaceful meadow beyond the canyon.

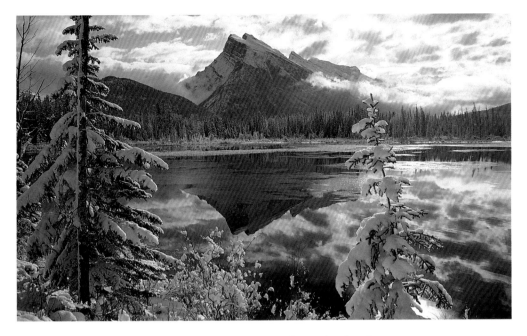

Rundle's cliffs are popular with rock climbers in summer
and waterfall ice climbers in winter.

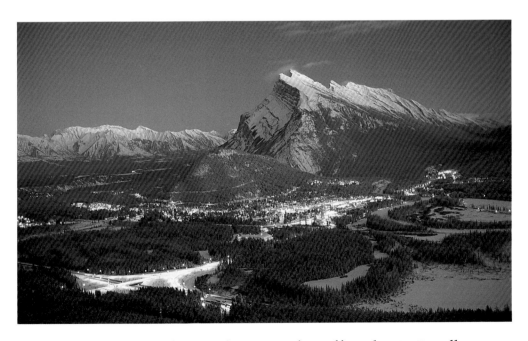

Winter dusk over the town of Banff, with Mt. Rundle
and Tunnel Mountain.

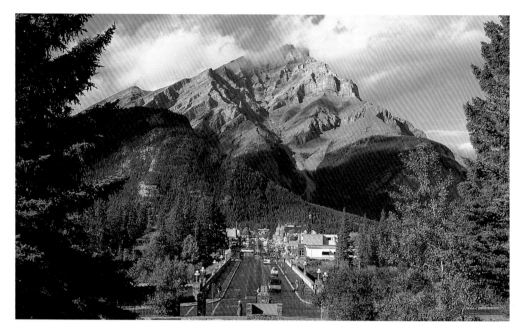

Wherever you go in the town of Banff,
Cascade Mountain goes also.

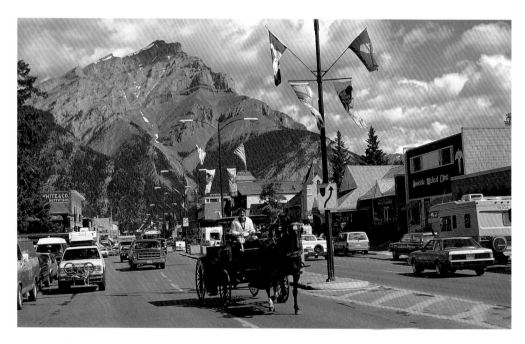

On hot summer days – and nights – Banff is the most vibrant
and exciting town in the Canadian Rockies.

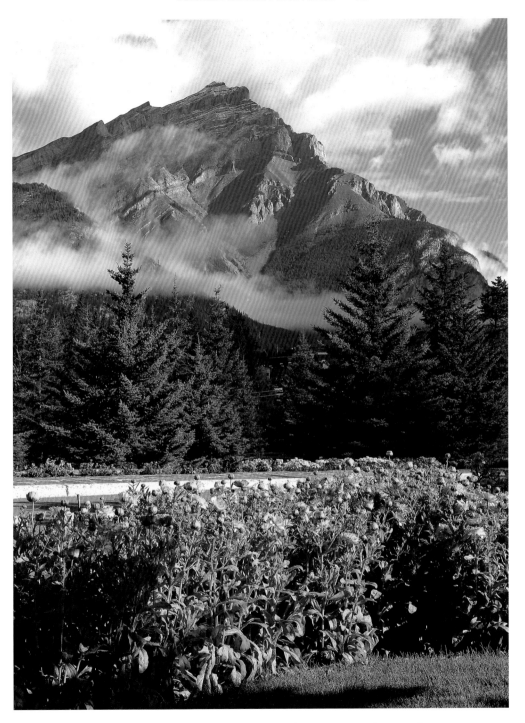

Cascade Mountain as seen from Cascade Gardens
at the Administration Building.

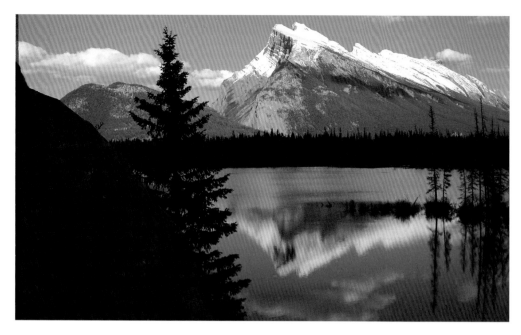

On this perfect summer day the massive cliffs of Mt. Rundle
are mirrored in the waters of the Vermilion Lakes.

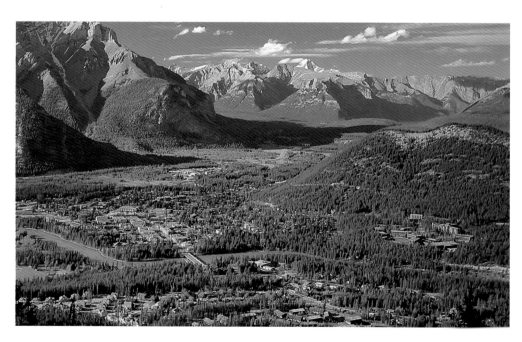

This view of the town of Banff and Cascade Mountain is from
Sulphur Mountain, where a heart-stopping gondola ride whisks
you to an elevation of 2285 metres in minutes.

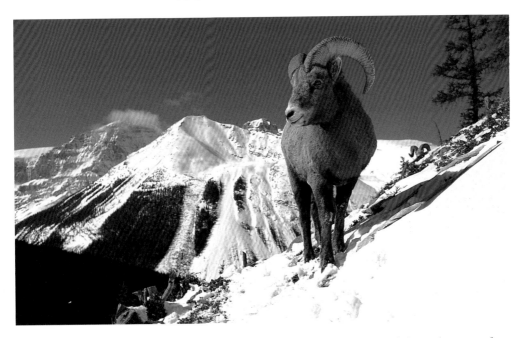

The jagged cliffs are the bighorn sheep's home turf, but during the rutting season the rams' ferocious head-butting contests will take them to level ground.

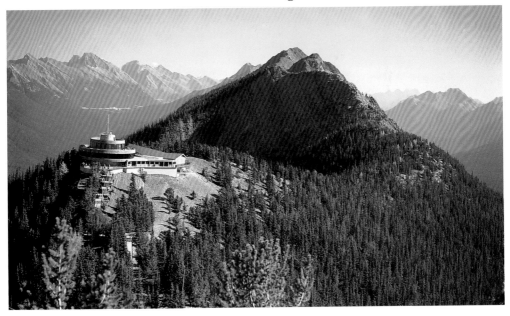

The Sulphur Mountain gondola takes you to this Upper Terminal, and a gorgeous view of the surrounding area.

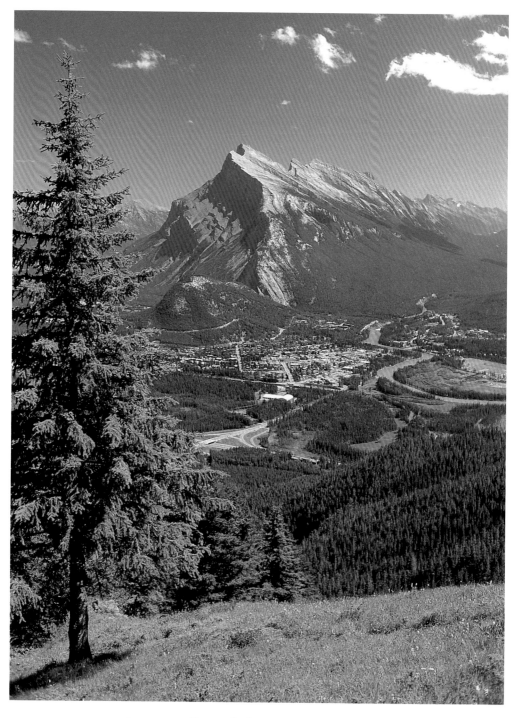

Mt. Rundle and the Town of Banff
from Mt. Norquay.

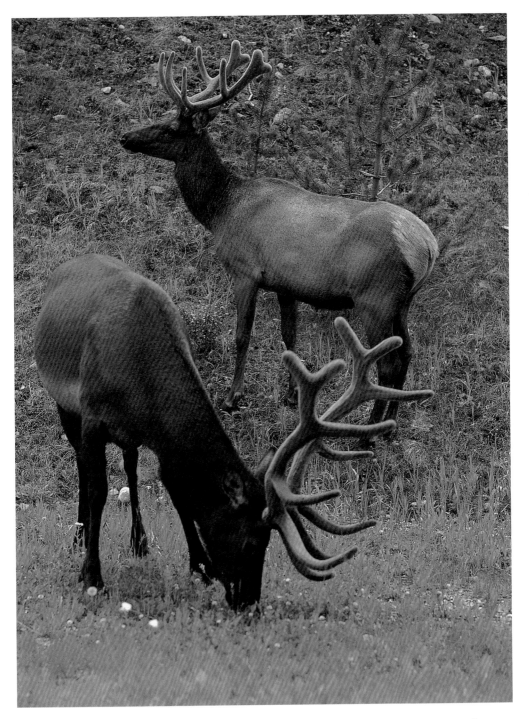

Male elk are famous for the violent antler-locking contests they engage in during mating season – the rut – each autumn.

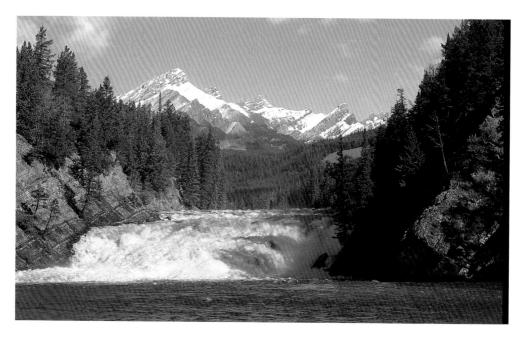

Even in the height of summer you can find solitude by
taking a stroll along the Bow River to Bow Falls.

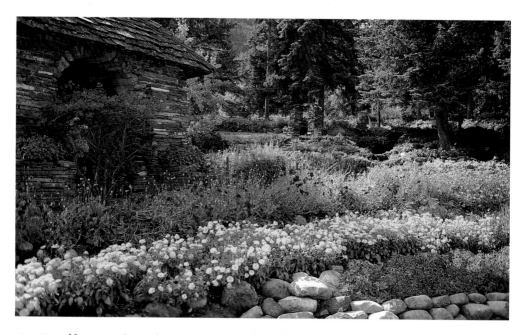

In Banff even the administration buildings have charming gardens,
complete with welcoming benches, for visitors to enjoy.

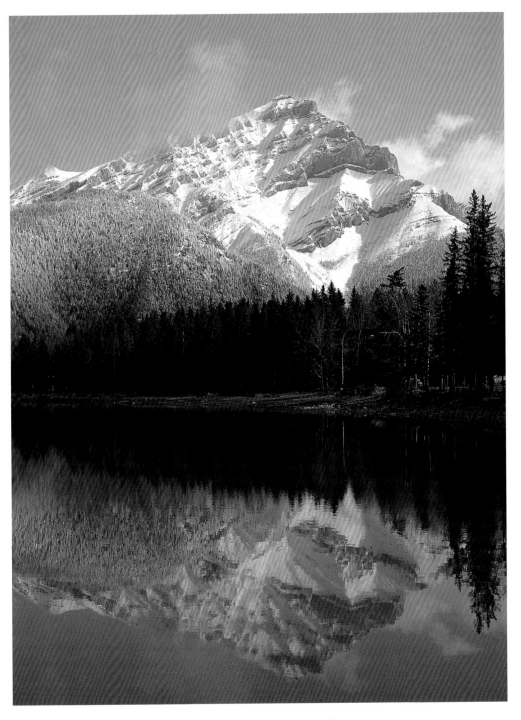

Draped in fresh snow, Cascade Mountain
is reflected in the Bow River.

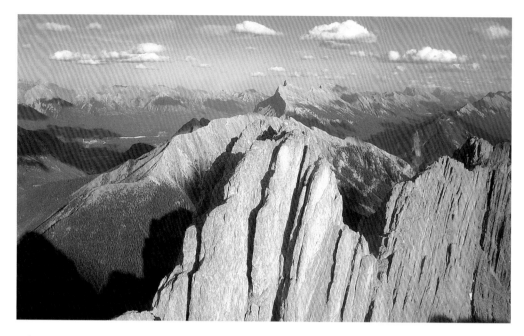

These climbers have conquered Mt. Louis, which is a classic example
of a dogtooth mountain. Mt. Rundle is visible in the distance.

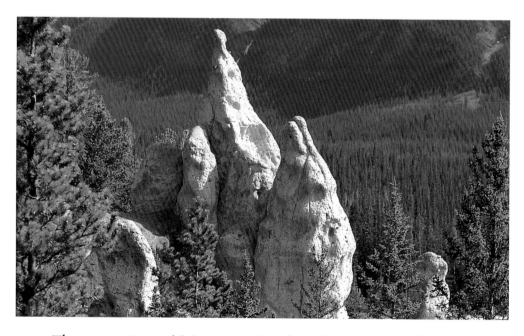

The exotic Tunnel Mountain Hoodoos have been sculpted
by water from deposits of glacial rubble.

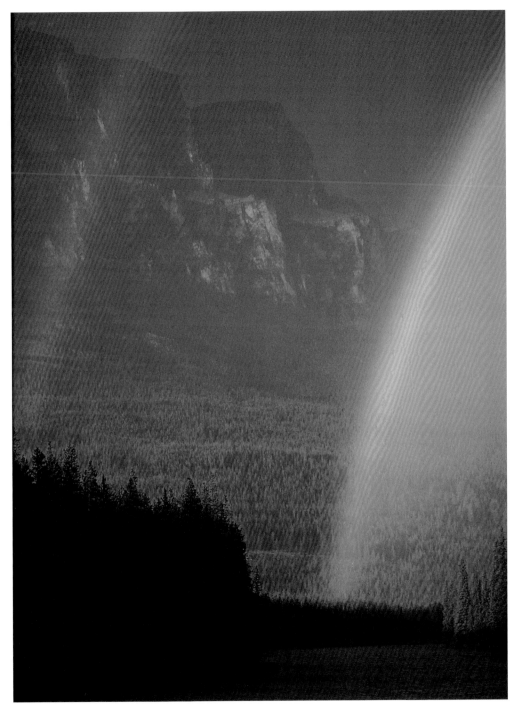

A double rainbow, captured forever on film,
at Castle Mountain.

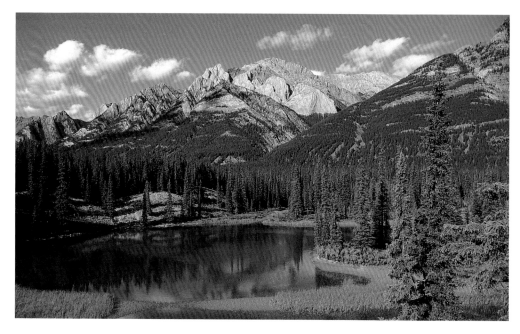

The jagged ridges of the Sawback Range parallel
the Bow Valley on the way to Lake Louise.

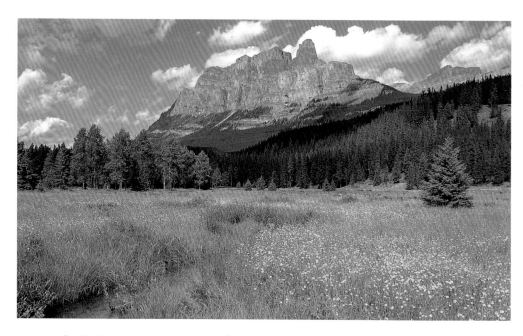

Of all the names bestowed in the Rockies, Castle Mountain
is one of the most appropriate. The cliffs of Castle are
very popular with rock climbers.

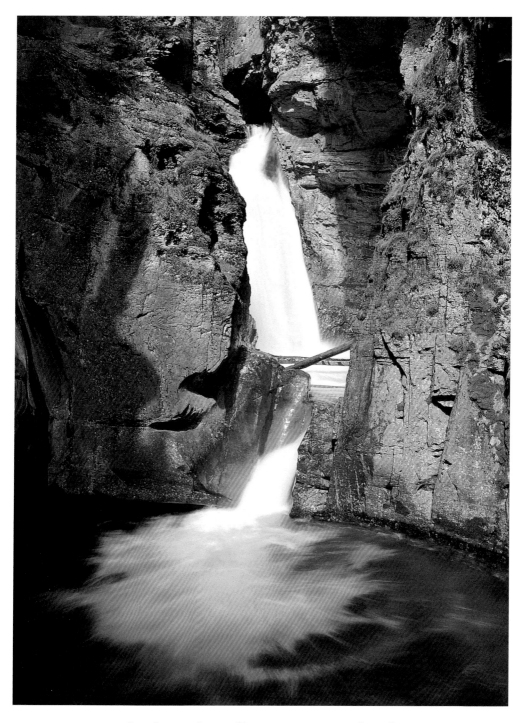

Thanks to the walkway constructed within it,
Johnston Canyon is one of the best places in the Rockies
to appreciate a limestone canyon.

Lake Louise

Only an occasional birdcall breaks
the mountain silence. Perhaps without
intending to do so, people find themselves
talking in hushed voices.

When a Stoney Indian guide took him to see the Lake of Little Fishes in 1883 Tom Wilson found a spectacle so majestic and moving that he thought he could improve upon the Native name: he christened his discovery Emerald Lake for its startling colour.

The lake was eventually named after Princess Louise Caroline Alberta, daughter of Queen Victoria and wife of Canada's Governor-General, and its fame spread rapidly. In 1890 the CPR built a modest chalet on the lakeshore facing Mt. Victoria. By the end of the century the chalet had expanded to a two-storey frame building, which became the centre for climbing expeditions by adventurers from near and far.

In 1924 the first Chateau Lake Louise was almost totally destroyed by fire, and was replaced by the present structure. With the addition of the Glacier Wing in 1986, the hotel can now accommodate up to 1000 guests. Its grounds are open to the public so that all visitors can enjoy the lake they call a 'diamond in the wilderness.' In 1918 the editor of the *Banff Crag and Canyon* wrote:

Nobody ever gets accustomed to Lake Louise. You come down in the morning, thinking of canteloupe and coffee. At the stairhead you have your first – yes, it is a smashing glimpse of the lake.

In the spring, blooms of all shapes and colours sprout from garden beds by the lakeshore and along well-groomed walkways. Only an occasional birdcall breaks the mountain silence. Perhaps without intending to do so, people find themselves talking in hushed voices.

By early fall the first snows come to Lake Louise, and with them the first skiers to test the slopes and trails in the vast ski area across Bow Valley from the lake. Many head for Skoki Lodge, a small log building built on the valley's eastern rim by cross-country enthusiasts in the early 1930's. Lake Louise is one of Canada's largest ski areas, covering 28 sq km /11 sq mi with over 40 marked runs.

Over the years, some 68 km/42 mi of hiking trails have been carved through the timber and over the rock surrounding Lake Louise. One of the most popular is a 5.5 km/3.4 mi hike to the teahouse at the Plain of Six Glaciers, where there's a splendid view of Mt. Lefroy, The Mitre and Mt. Victoria. Another popular trail winds steeply up to the teahouse at Lake Agnes via Mirror Lake and Bridal Veil Falls.

Down the road from Lake Louise, about 12 km/7.5 mi to the south, lies Moraine Lake, a gem-like lake set in the Valley of the Ten Peaks. Like other glacial lakes, its colour changes with the weather and the seasons, ranging from dark blue to an almost unbelievable blue-green at the time of maximum run-off. Explorer Walter Wilcox once said of Moraine Lake, 'No scene has given me an equal impression of inspiring solitude and rugged grandeur.' The ten peaks are now officially called the Wenkchemna Peaks.

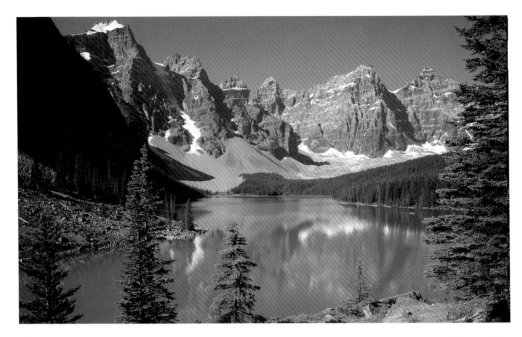

Of all the heavenly sights in the Canadian Rockies, Moraine Lake and the Wenkchemna Peaks is one of the loveliest. It was probably chosen to appear on the back of our twenty-dollar bill for that very reason.

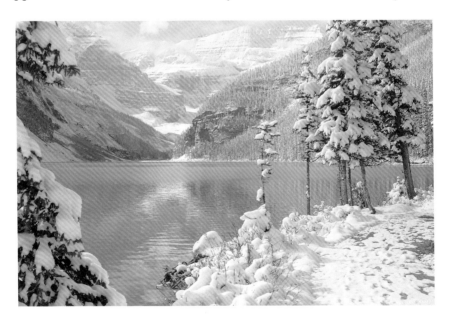

Some think Lake Louise is at its most
beautiful in the dead of winter.

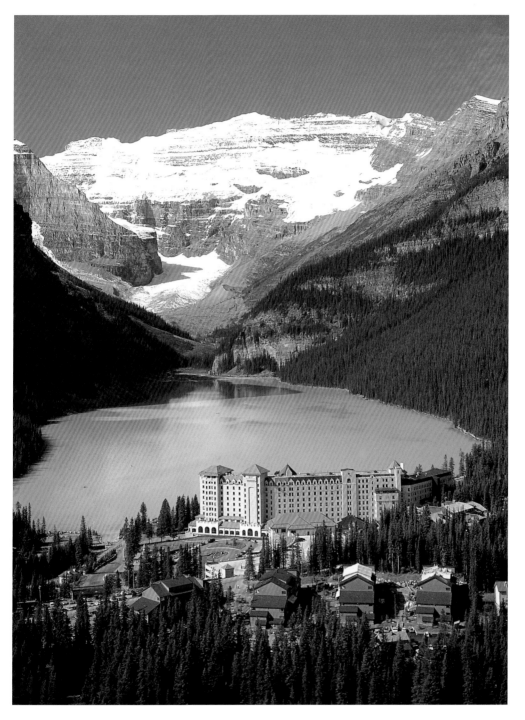

The green-blue of Lake Louise is so extraordinary that people sometimes suspect that photos like this one have been retouched – until they see the lake for themselves.

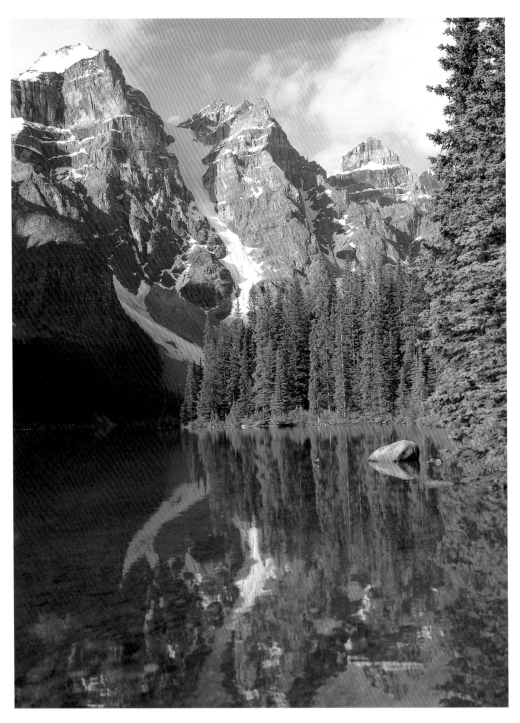

The best time to photograph Moraine Lake is at dawn on a still, clear morning, when the mountains are reflected in the water.

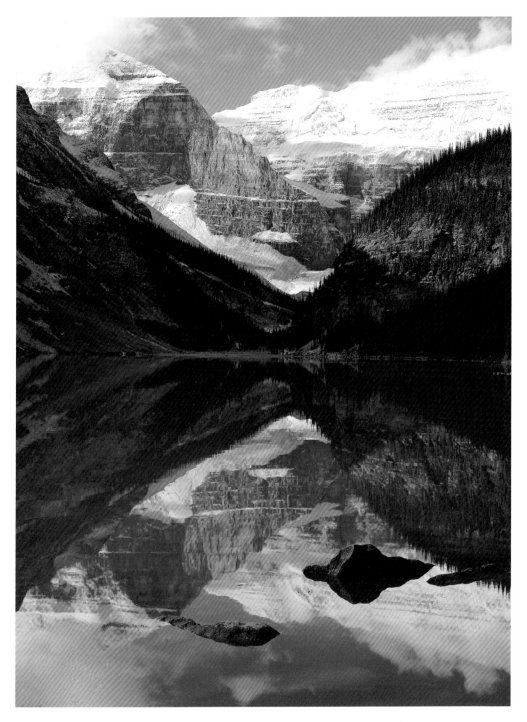

Mt. Lefroy (left) and Mt. Victoria,
reflected in Lake Louise.

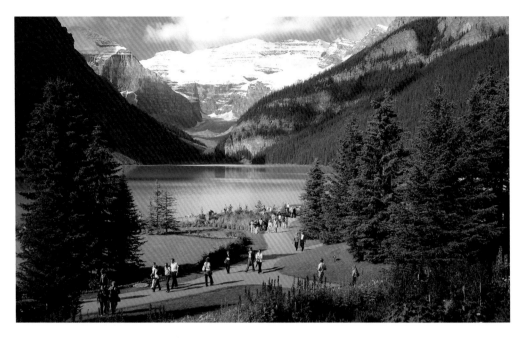

The Chateau's famous gardens include the Icelandic poppy, which is native to Siberia (and well-suited to short summers).

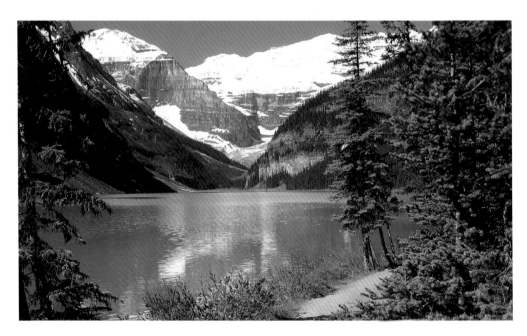

The trail at Lake Louise continues to the Plain of Six Glaciers, which is a popular destination for hikers.

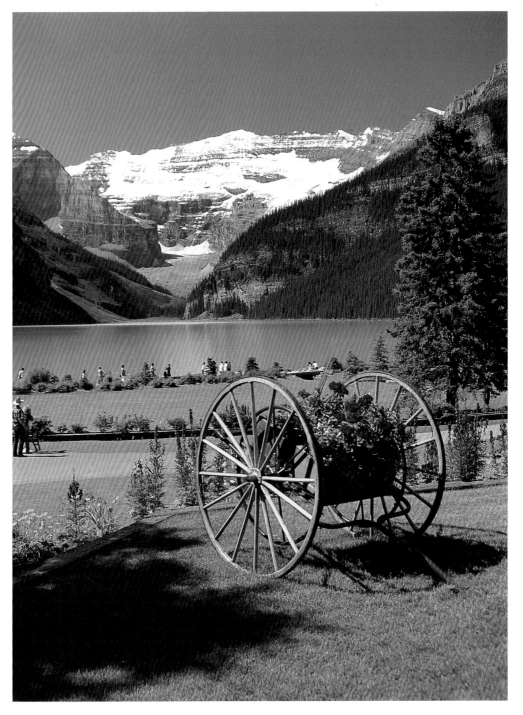

Most of the 'snow' on Mt. Victoria's steep flanks
is actually glacial ice, so it's there year-round.

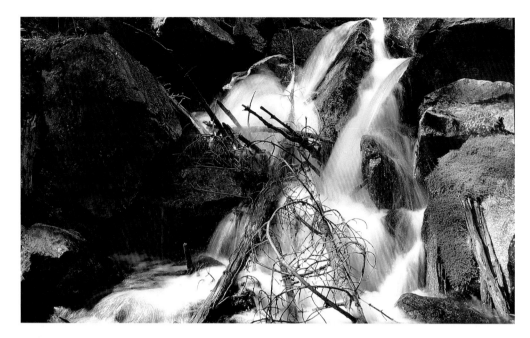

Bridal Veil Falls near Lake Agnes,
on the way to the teahouse.

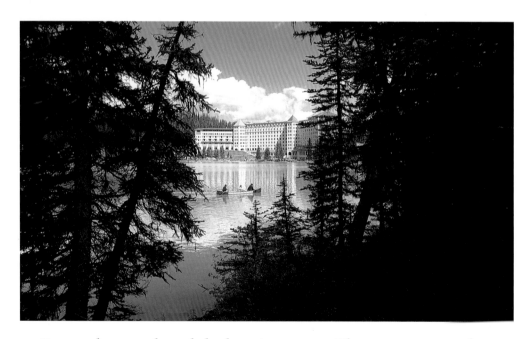

Escape the crowds and the heat in a canoe. The temperature of
Lake Louise never gets much above 4°c/7°c.

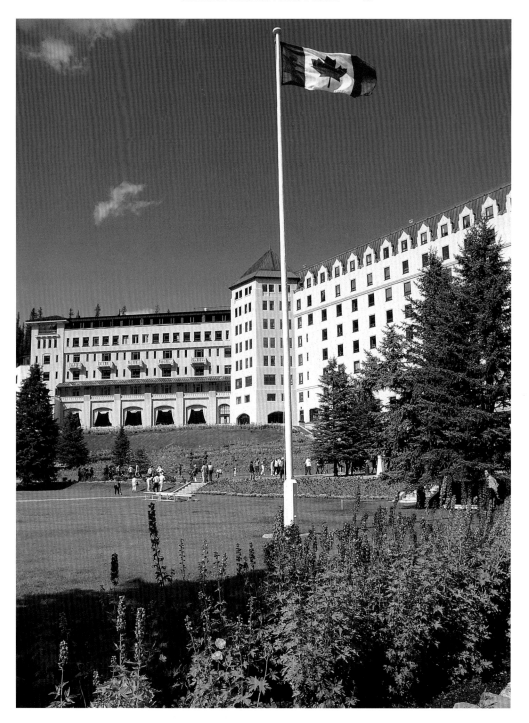

Redevelopment that began in 1986 has boosted the Chateau's
capacity to 1000 guests. The hotel is open year-round.

Yoho

Yoho is a Native Indian word
expressing awe, and it's an apt description
for this tiny mountain park.

His Stoney Indian guides thought Sir James Hector was a goner, for sure. An ornery pack horse had kicked him in the chest and knocked him cold. The Native guides were about to bury him forever in his beloved mountains when, to their great surprise, he suddenly came to. That was in 1858. Sir James recovered to continue his expedition of discovery, and that's how Kicking Horse River and the Kicking Horse Pass got their names.

The Kicking Horse River bisects Yoho National Park, the smallest and, some say, the prettiest of Canada's four Rocky Mountain parks. Yoho is a Native Indian word expressing awe, and it's an apt description. Much of the park's 1313 sq km/507 sq mi area is inaccessible to all but the most intrepid mountaineer. Massive peaks soar above a maze of lakes, rivers, forest valleys and steep canyons.

Some historians wonder why the CPR chose this route for the first trans-continental track through the mountains, since other less challenging routes were available. It was an engineering accomplishment of heroic magnitude, but scores of workers lost their lives. The story is graphically told in an exhibit atop the pass. The railway was completed in 1884, and the highway followed in 1927.

Yoho's theme is 'rockwalls and waterfalls,' and it has plenty of both. The eastern part of the park features glaciers, icefields, lakes and the high peaks of the Continental Divide. The drier, warmer western area included the broad valley of the Kicking Horse River and abundant wildlife.

The Burgess Shale, one of the world's most fascinating fossil beds, is located on the slopes of Mt. Stephen at Field, BC and near Burgess Pass above Emerald Lake. Some of the fossilized remains of marine animals found here date back 530 million years. The Burgess Shale was designated a World Heritage Site in 1980, and the fossil beds are protected.

Another highlight of Yoho National Park is Emerald Lake. Surrounded by tall timber and taller mountains, this beautiful green-blue lake sits in quiet splendour about 8 km/5 mi from the highway, just west of Field. Boating, fishing, swimming, hiking and cross-country skiing are popular activities in the area.

Emerald Lake Lodge and Conference Centre, a year-round resort that attracts vacationers and business travellers from around the world, sits on a hill overlooking the lake. Some 200 people can be accommodated in 85 guest units, in the main lodge and in two- and four-person cabins. The original Emerald Lake Lodge was built by the CPR in 1902 of hand-hewn timber and, despite renovations in 1986, the Lodge still blends in with its surroundings. No new development has been permitted in the area since the 1920's.

Rivalling Emerald as the most beautiful of lakes in Yoho is Lake O'Hara, which mountaineer James Outram described as 'the fairest of mountain lakelet tarns' in 1900. Ever since this and other accounts praising the beauty of Lake O'Hara appeared, countless other visitors have arrived and agreed.

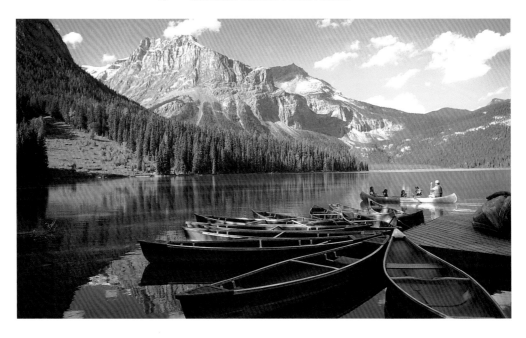

Hiking, fishing, trail riding and canoeing are popular activities
at Emerald Lake in Yoho National Park.

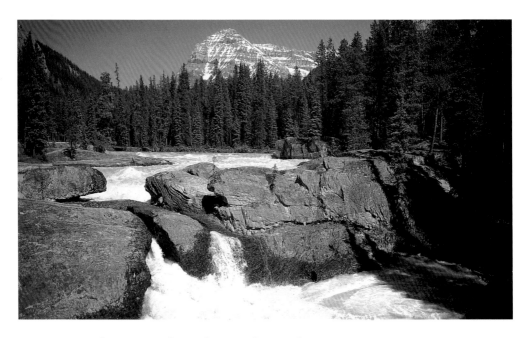

The Natural Bridge in the Kicking Horse River,
with Mt. Stephen in the background.

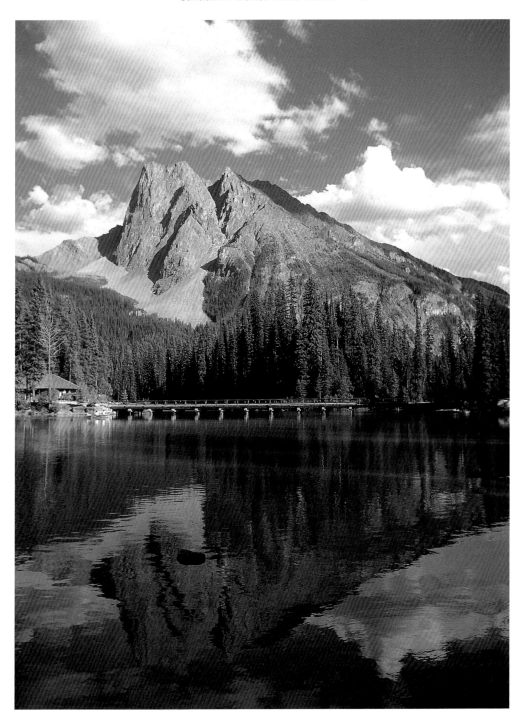

Mt. Burgess and Emerald Lake.
The east side of Emerald lake has been declared
a world heritage site, for its unique flowers and plants.

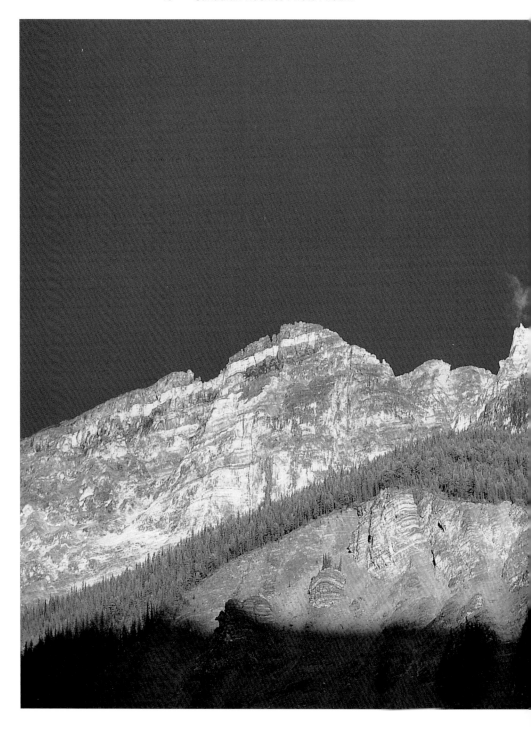

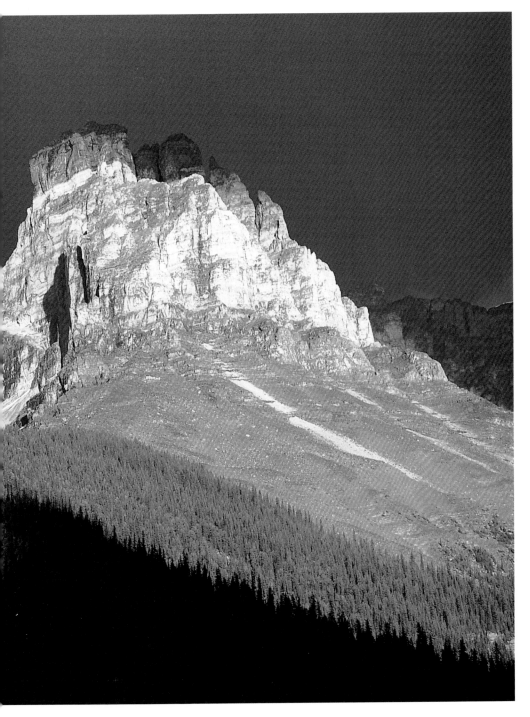

Cathedral Mountain towers over the Trans-Canada Highway
at the bottom of Yoho's 'Big Hill.'

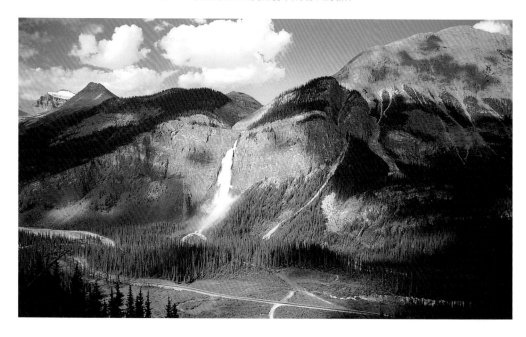

Takakkaw Falls and the Yoho Valley. These falls are named
for the Native expression 'it is wonderful!'

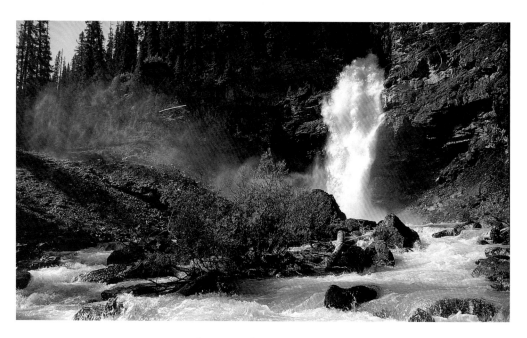

On sunny days early morning visitors
may see a rainbow in Laughing Falls.

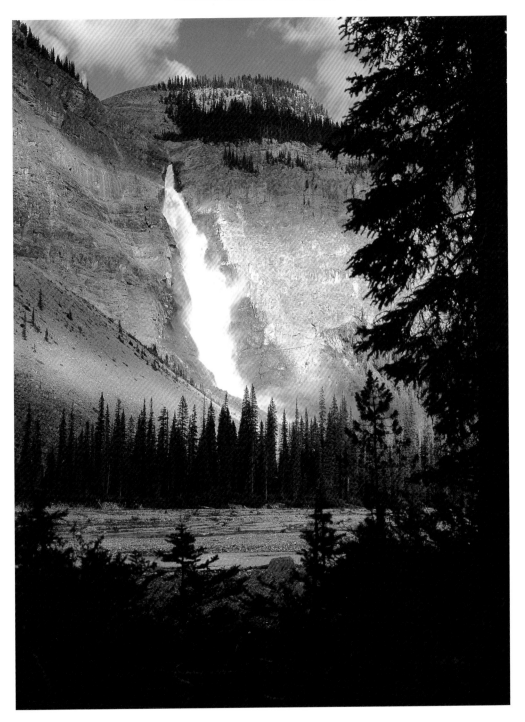

Takakkaw Falls is one of
the highest waterfalls in Canada.

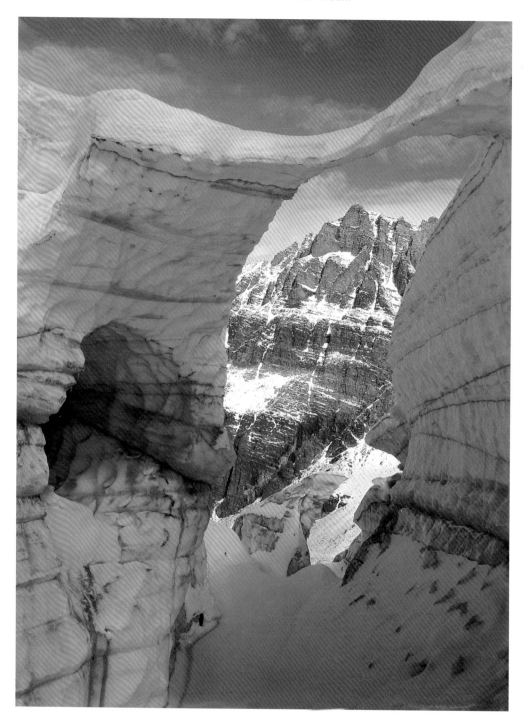

Snow Bridge near Lake O'Hara.

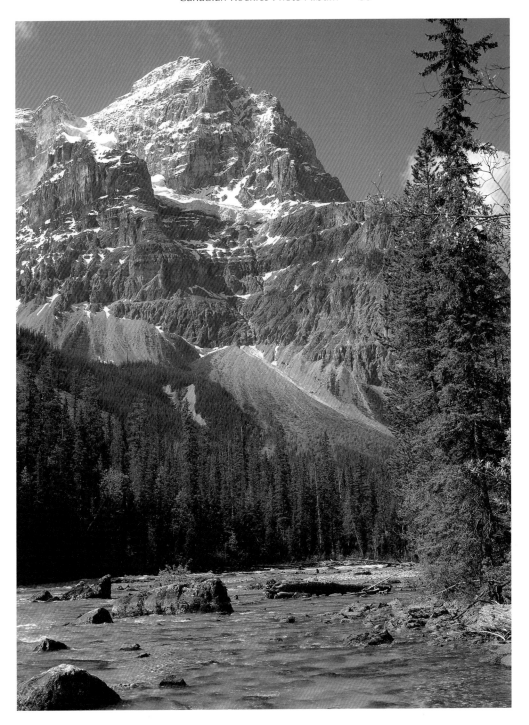

Lofty Mt. Stephen dominates the Kicking Horse Valley
in the vicinity of Field, BC.

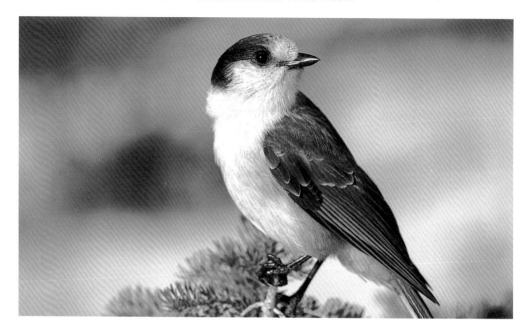

The gray jay's nickname is whisky jack, adapted from
the Cree 'wis-kat-jon.' Its cousin is the Clark's nutcracker.

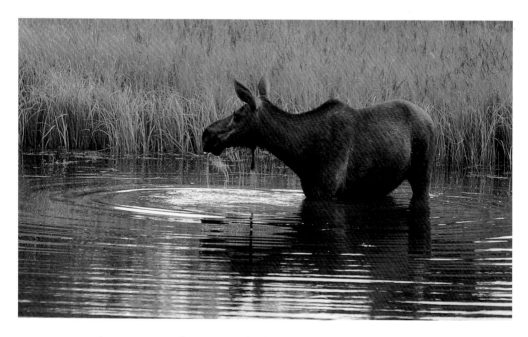

The moose's favourite habitat frequently occurs
at roadside along the Icefields Parkway, so visitors stand
a chance of seeing this reclusive creature.

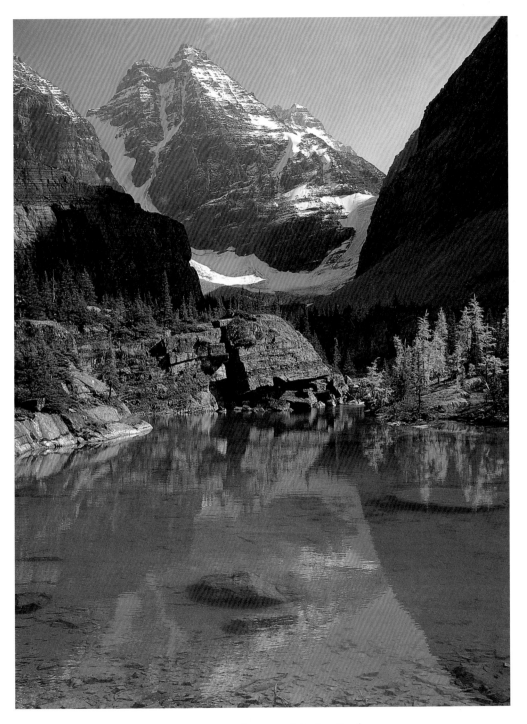

Mt. Hungabee and Lake Lefroy.

Kootenay

No other park in Canada can boast of having both cactus and glacier within its borders.

Though it's only slightly larger than neighbouring Yoho, Kootenay is a park of tremendous diversity, incorporating both mountain and valley climates, four distinct mountain topographies and hundreds of species of animals and plants. No other park in Canada can boast of having both cactus and glacier within its borders, and only Banff National Park has more visitors in a year.

At its northern end Kootenay features jagged peaks similar to others along the spine of the Continental Divide. Gradually the mountains become more gentle, the forests thicker, the valleys greener and wider.

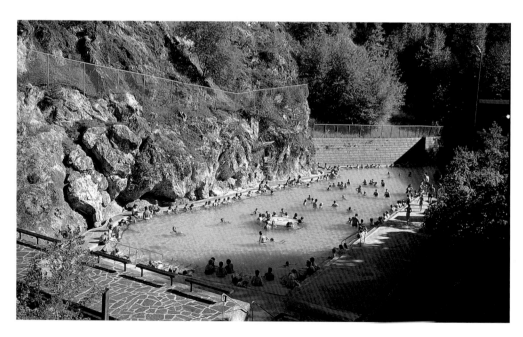

Unlike others in the Rockies, the Radium Hot Springs are virtually odourless, and they're good and hot.

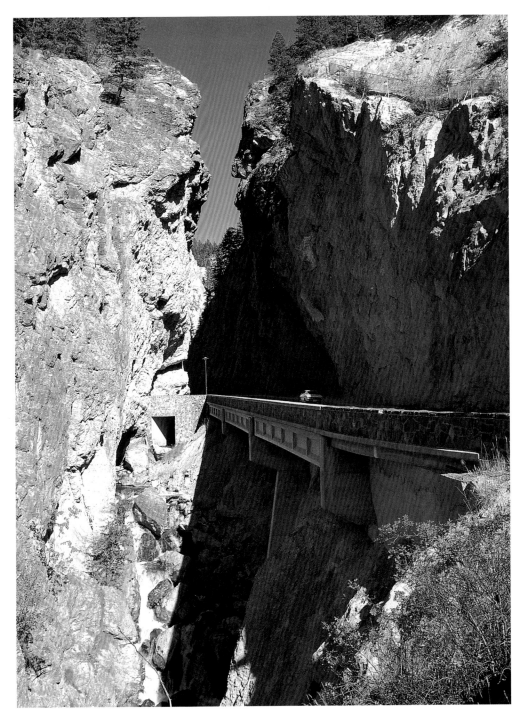

The Edge of the Rockies trail explores the creek bed near
the mouth of Sinclair Canyon in Kootenay National Park.

The Icefields Parkway

'A constant flow of travel will demand a broad, well-ballasted motor road ... this wonder trail will be world-renowned.'

The now-famous Icefields Parkway, completed in the 1960's, replaced the bumpy, twisty Banff-Jasper Highway, which had been built as a relief project during the Depression. As it climbs toward the summit of Bow Pass, magnificent icefields sculpted by millions of years of glacial action come into view. This is certainly one of the most enchanting drives in the world.

In 1920 surveyor A. O. Wheeler wrote:

Through dense primeval forests, muskeg, burnt and fallen timber and along rough and steeply sloping hillsides, a constant flow of travel will demand a broad, well-ballasted motor road ... this wonder trail will be world-renowned.

And it is. The Parkway was first used by cars in 1940, and echoing the words mountaineer Edward Whymper spoke forty years earlier, was heralded in the *Banff Crag and Canyon* as being 'twenty Switzerlands in one.'

All along the route of this incredible highway, from Banff to The Crossing to Columbia Icefield to Jasper, the scenery is exquisite. Just when you think you've seen the most beautiful blue-ice glacier you're ever going to see, an even more dazzling one looms into view.

In the journey north from Lake Louise, the crossing of

the North Saskatchewan River was the biggest obstacle facing explorers on horseback. Many expeditions were cut short because of supplies lost in the river when horses were submerged. When construction of the parkway got underway in the 1930's, the crossing of this river again posed an immense problem.

Many travellers today cross the bridge at 'The Crossing' unaware of the drama that unfolded in the past. Most, however, do find time to stop at The Crossing Resort on the north side of the river, to buy souvenirs.

In *A Tramp Abroad*, Mark Twain said:

A man who keeps company with glaciers comes to feel tolerably insignificant by and by. The mountains and glaciers together are able to take every bit of conceit out of a man and reduce his self-importance to zero if he will only remain within the influence of their sublime presence long enough to give it a fair and reasonable chance to do its work.

As you stand at the toe of the Athabasca Glacier, the immensity of the Columbia Icefield is almost beyond comprehension. This canopy of interlocking glaciers spreads over 337 sq km/130 sq mi of land, and in places it's close to 305 m/1000 ft thick. Only skilled climbers and guided tours venture out onto its ever-changing surface, which is a complex and beautiful mix of crevasses, icefalls, meltwater streams and ice of a dozen hues.

The history of the glaciers is explained at the Icefield Centre operated by Parks Canada, next to the chalet. A bit farther along you'll find the snowmobile-bus depot. Athabasca Glacier, the glacier closest to the Icefield Centre, is framed by Mt. Athabasca on the left and Mt. Kitchener on the right.

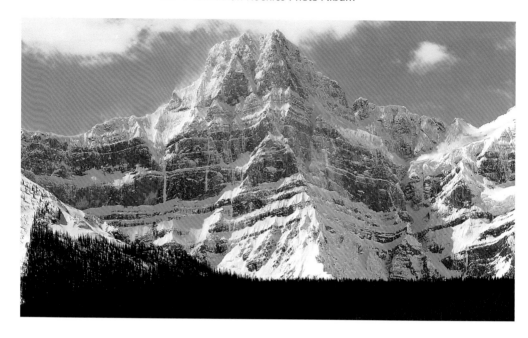

The Canadian Rockies are famous for glacier-studded, snow-capped mountains like Howse Peak in Banff National Park.

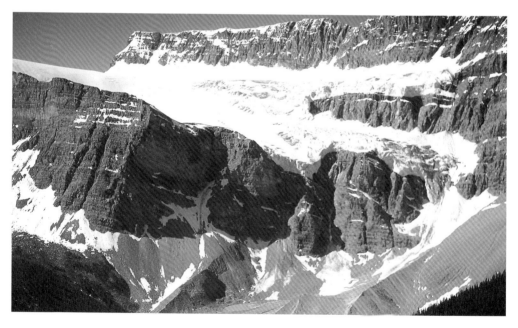

When Crowfoot Glacier was named it hadn't yet receded, and had three toes instead of just two.

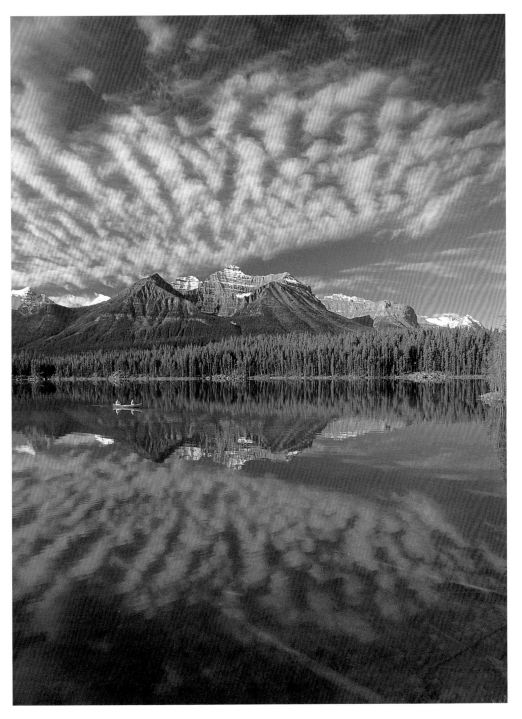

For a few weeks in summer when its waters are warm enough,
locals use Herbert Lake near Lake Louise as a swimming hole.

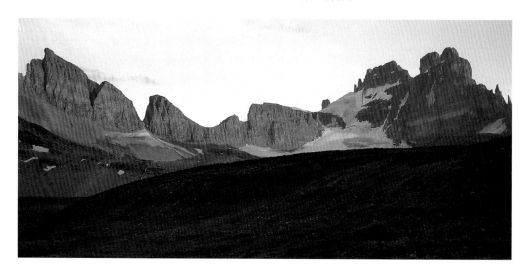

Sunset on Dolomite Peak.

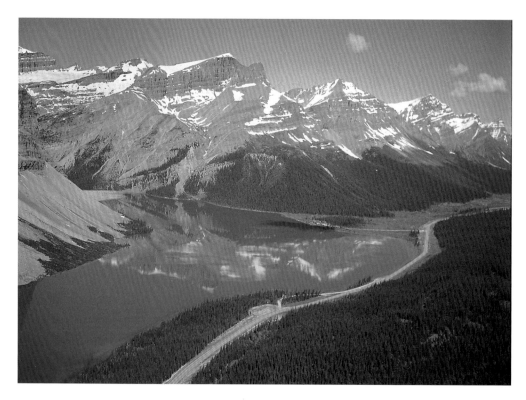

The Icefields Parkway travels next to Bow Lake,
from which Bow River flows.

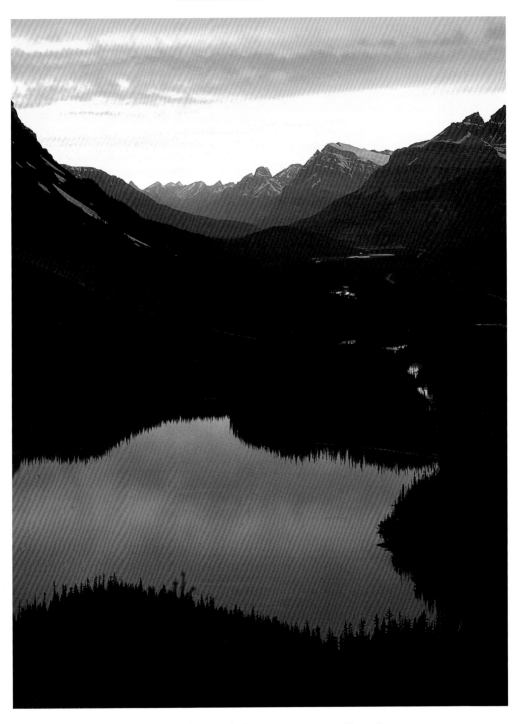

Peyto Lake and the Mistaya Valley during
a particularly lovely August sunset.

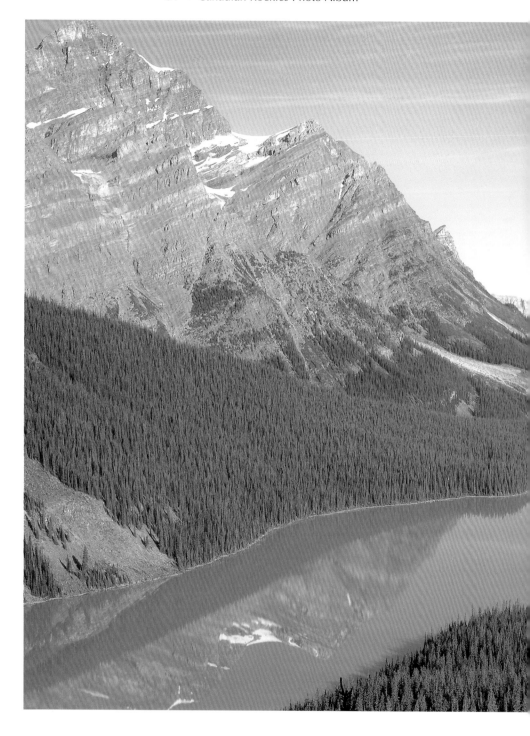

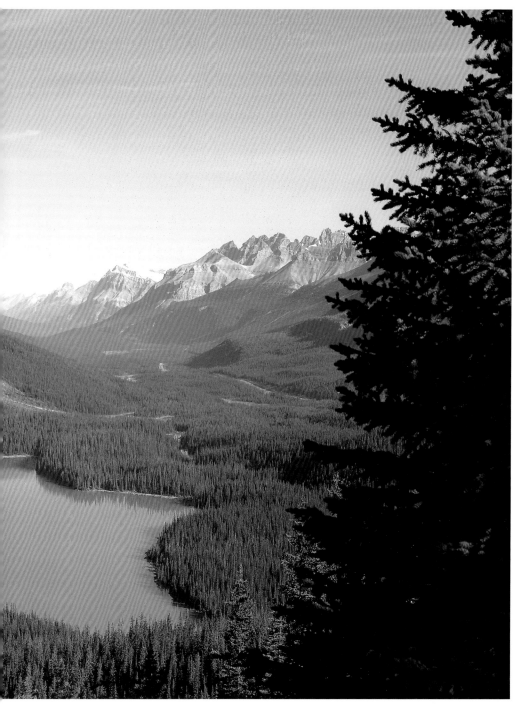

Peyto Lake is renowned for its distinctive
turquoise colour and unusual shape.

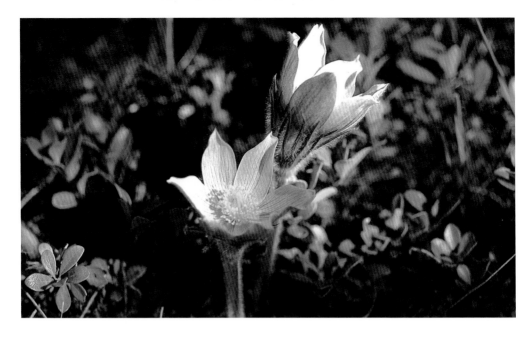

The crocus is one of many lovely flowers
at home in the Rockies.

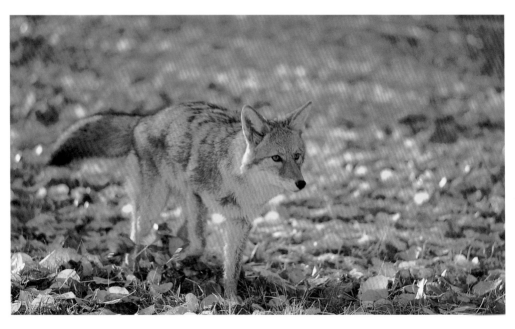

Although they are mostly seen alone or in pairs,
coyotes occasionally band together to hunt larger game –
especially in winter.

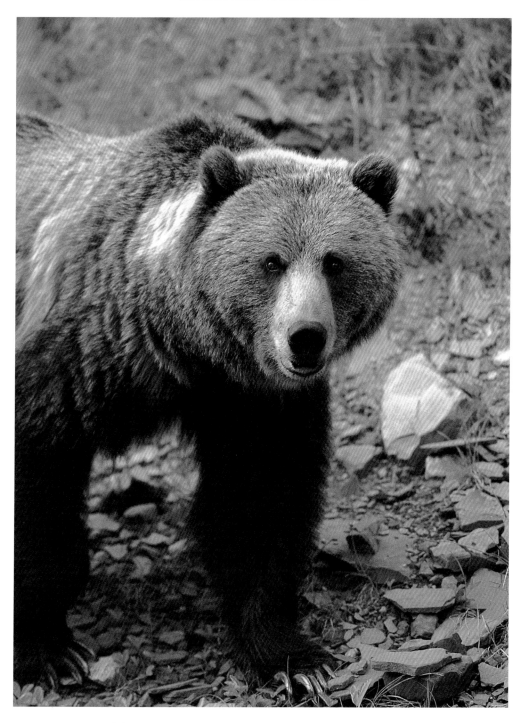

Although the grizzly bear is the dominant animal
in the Rockies, it's not much of a hunter –
its diet is about 90% vegetarian.

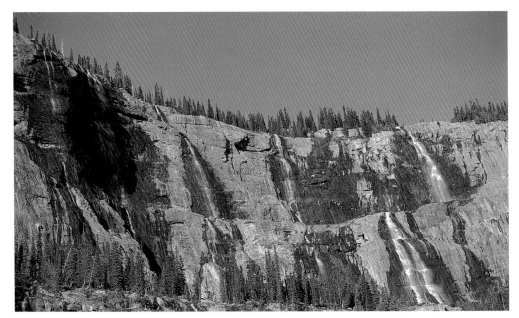

The waterfalls for which The Weeping Wall in Banff
National Park are named are the product of melting snow
high up on Cirrus Mountain.

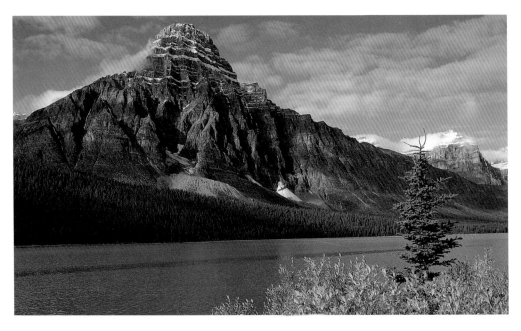

The rock of pyramid-like Mt. Chephren, reflected here in the
Waterfowl Lakes, is over 500 million years old.

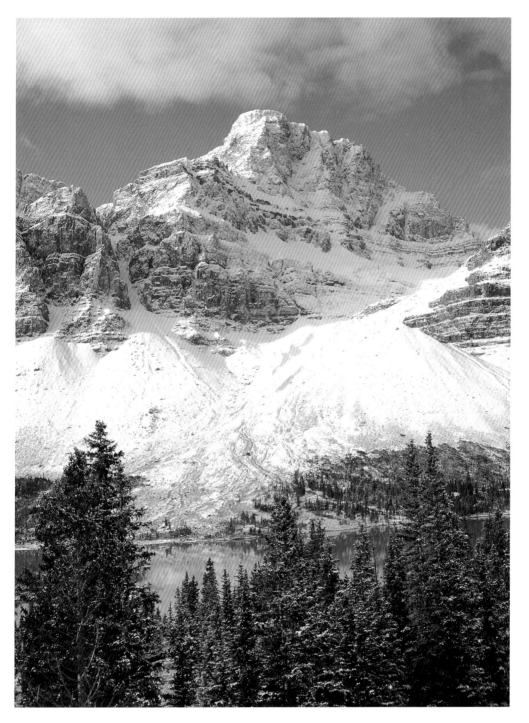

The massive upper cliff of Crowfoot Mountain
is a natural snow fence that deposits snow on
the plateau beneath – and on Crowfoot Glacier.

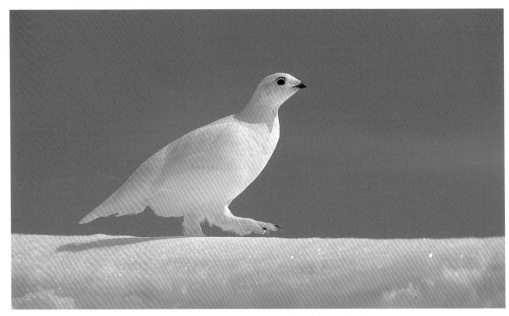

The white-tailed ptarmigan sheds and changes
its feathers to match the snow in winter, and the mottled
colours of boulderfields in summer.

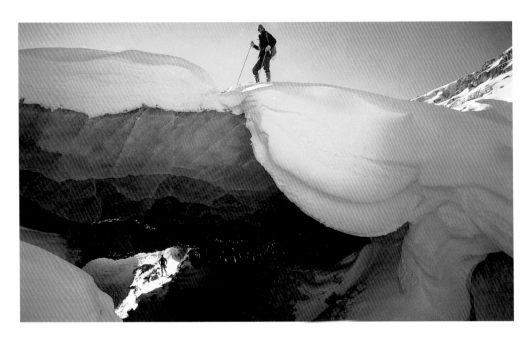

Ice Bridge at Saskatchewan Glacier, where
the powerful Saskatchewan River is born.

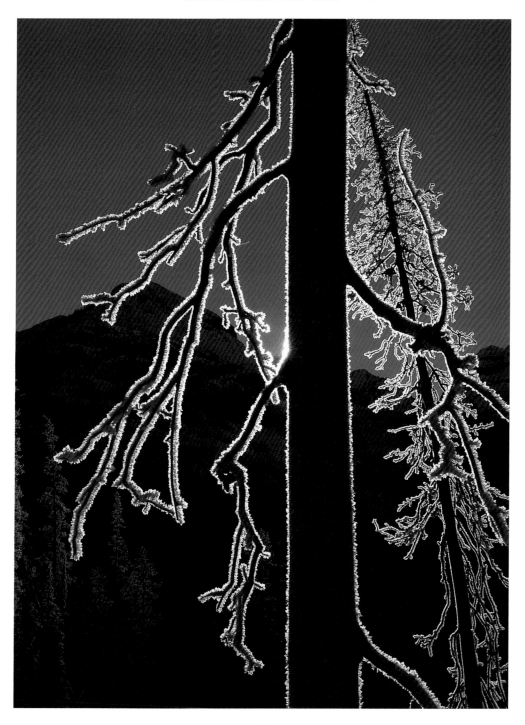

A hoar-frosted tree
glistens in the winter sun.

Wandering on to Jasper

Bighorn sheep are a common sight between Athabasca Glacier and Sunwapta Falls. This area is avalanche and rock slide country. At a number of points along the highway, barren swaths can be seen on the mountainsides across the Sunwapta Valley, where forests have been obliterated by hundreds of thousands of tons of crashing snow. Near the Jonas Creek Campground, a jumbled mass of pinkish boulders covers a vast area on both sides of the road, the result of a gigantic rock slide that thundered down from the ridge to the east.

Between Sunwapta Falls and Jasper, you'll see some of the giants of the Canadian Rockies: Mt. Kerkeslin and Brussels Peak, both about 3050 m/10,000 ft; Mt. Fryatt and Mt. Edith Cavell, each over 3350 m/11,000 ft. The latter is home to the captivating Angel Glacier.

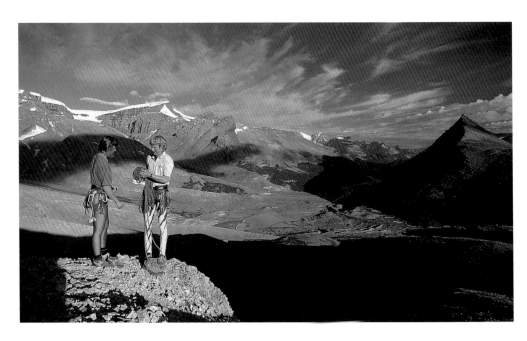

When you see the sort of view that climbing rewards its followers with, it's much easier to appreciate their passion for the sport.

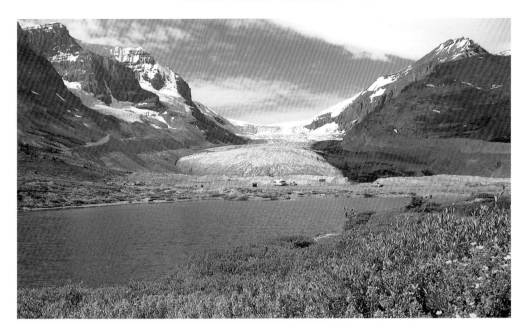

Glaciers like the Athabasca store over 90% of
the world's fresh water in frozen form.

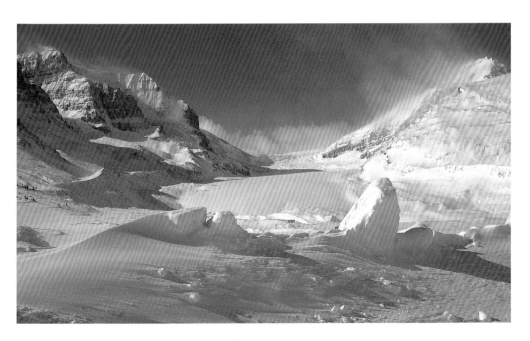

Athabasca Glacier in the wintertime.

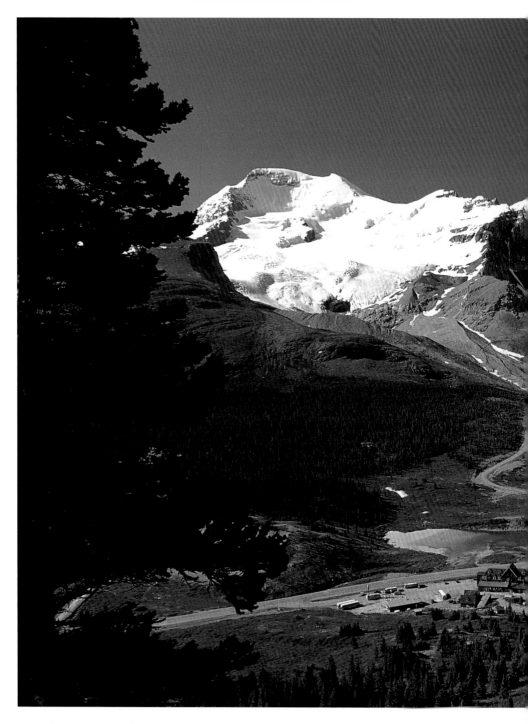

At the turn of the century, Athabasca Glacier flowed right through the valley the Icefields Parkway now travels through.

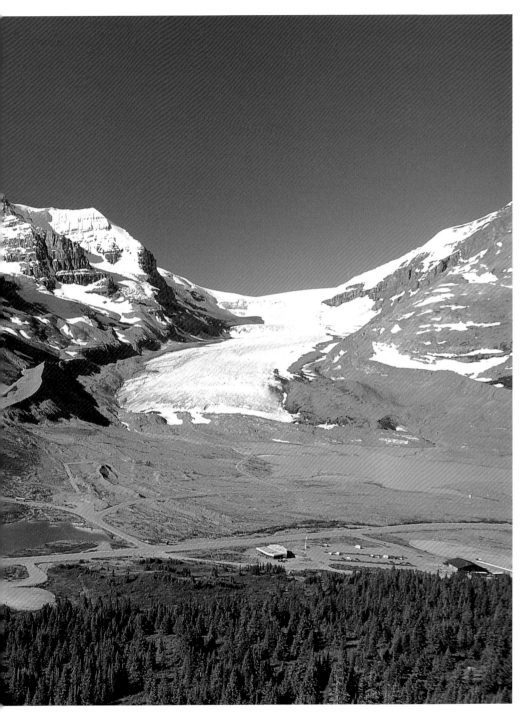

As the glaciers shrink,
so does the world's freshwater reservoir.

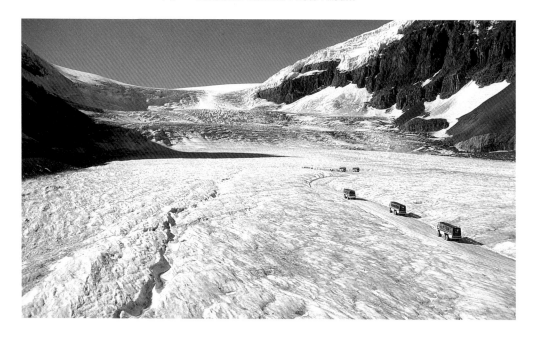

Snowcoaches make their way
onto the toe of Athabasca Glacier.

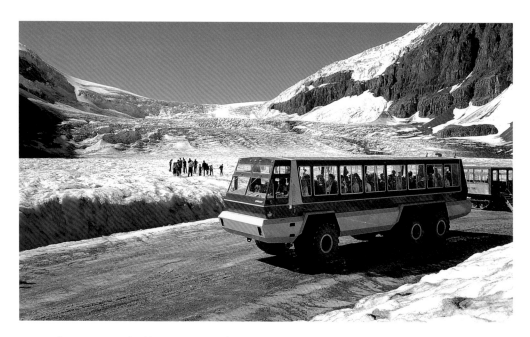

This type of all-terrain vehicle has been used to take visitors
onto Athabasca Glacier since 1981.

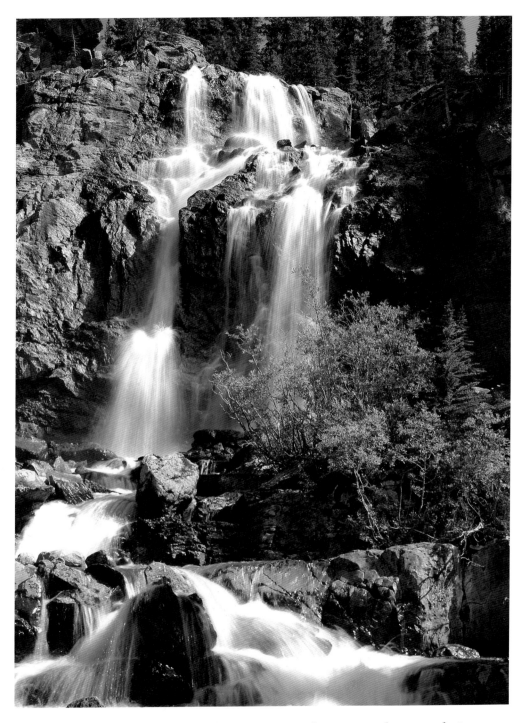

Untracked bush is known to outfitters as 'shin tangle,'
and Tangle Falls in Jasper National Park is named for it.

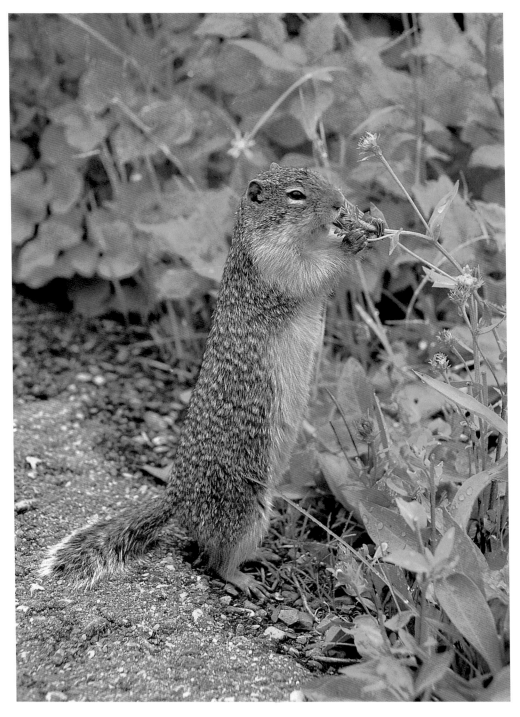

Columbian ground squirrels spend the summer fattening themselves up and stockpiling food, in preparation for hibernation.

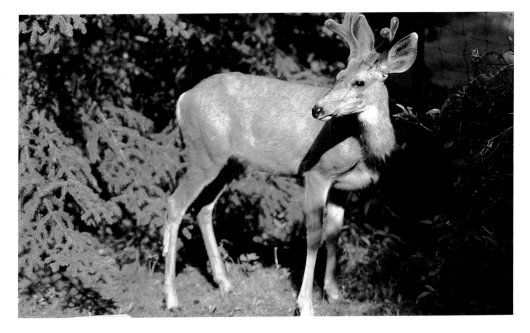

Mule deer are often sighted by visitors to the Rockies –
they enjoy nibbling on the shrubs in people's gardens.

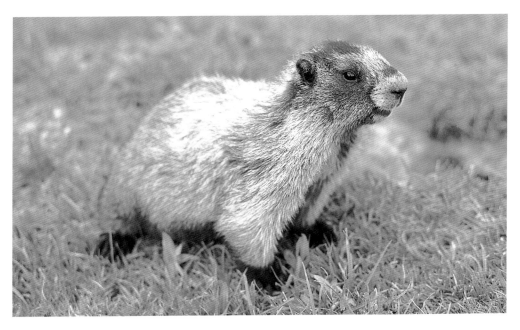

Hoary marmots are similar to woodchucks,
but they're about twice as big.

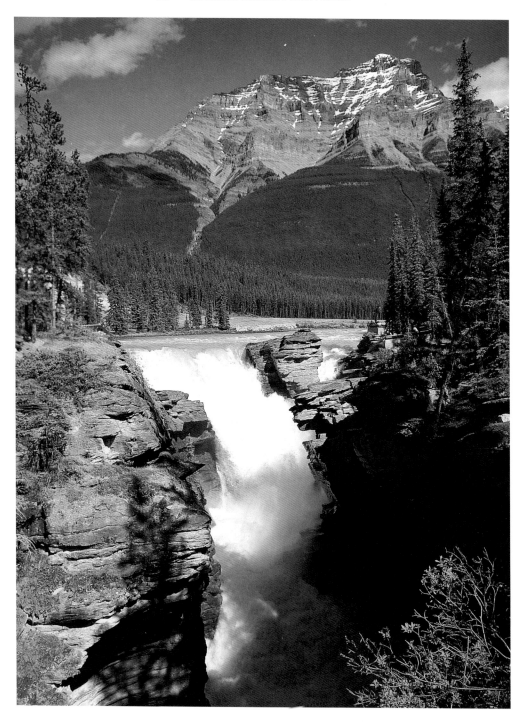

An interpretive walk offers close-up views
of Athabasca Falls in Jasper National Park.
That's Mt. Kerkeslin in the background.

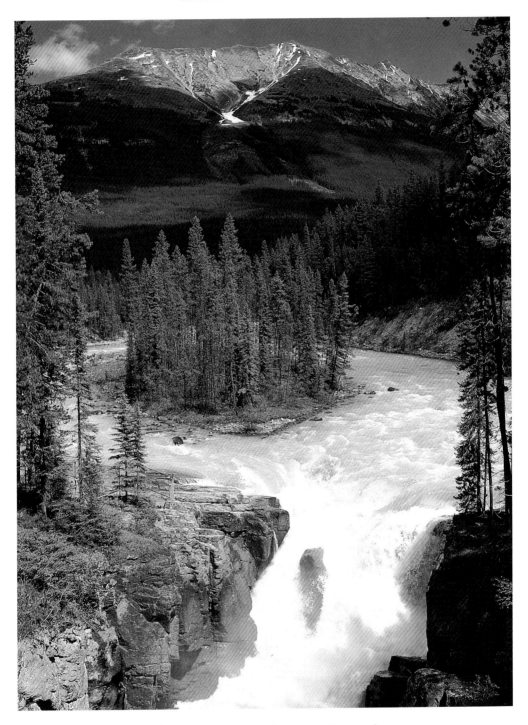

While the Athabasca Falls flow through quartzite,
the Sunwapta River has eroded Sunwapta Falls through cracks
in the underlying limestone.

Jasper

Countless well-groomed trails wind
through the thickly wooded mountainsides,
past lakes and streams.

*There she was, sure enough. No doubting the highest
peak in the Rockies of Canada – she spoke for herself. To
our weary, sunburnt eyes she loomed refreshingly up
from behind a hill, cold, icy, clean-cut, in a sky unclouded
and of intensest blue. The mountains rising far and near
were but worthy of the name of hills, leaving Robson a
noble massive vision to the pilgrims who had come so far
to see her.*
— Explorer Mary T. S. Schäffer, 1907

At 10,878 sq km, Jasper is the largest of the four mountain
parks, and the third most visited national park in Canada,
after Banff and Kootenay. Jasper deserves all those visitors, as this extraordinary wilderness area is home to
many of the best-known mountain park attractions in the
Rockies, including Maligne Lake and Spirit Island, Mt.
Edith Cavell, Mt. Robson, Medicine Lake, Roche Miette,
and the Miette Hot Springs (hottest in the Canadian
Rockies).

But this sprawling northern park is, above all else, a
land of lakes, many of which are popular with boaters,
swimmers, fishermen, birdwatchers and photographers.
Incredible as it may seem, there are over 800 lakes and
ponds in Jasper National Park.

Many of the small lakes near the townsite were created
by melting blocks of glacial ice at the end of the Wisconsin

Glaciation. Lac Beauvert, Edith Lake and Lake Annette originated in this manner. The area around the lakes is a fire succession forest of lodgepole pine, a product of the forest fires that consumed much of the forest in the Athabasca Valley in 1889.

Jasper is criss-crossed by a fabulous network of hiking trails over 1000 km long. Backpacking areas like the North Boundary Trail, Skyline Trail and Tonquin Valley offer the opportunity for adventure, and countless well groomed trails wind through the thickly wooded mountainsides, past lakes and streams where the fishing and swimming are great. Park naturalists conduct informative walking tours up in the mountains and down in the valleys.

The Pyramid Lake Road climbs onto a bench north of Jasper townsite, and gives access to two of the largest and most picturesque lakes in the region, Patricia Lake and Pyramid Lake. Along the way the road passes through a fire succession forest of lodgepole pine and trembling aspen, and contours along the edge of Cottonwood Slough, a montane wetland created by beaver dams. The slough is one of the best bird-watching areas in Jasper.

The upper terminal of the Jasper tramway provides a panoramic view of the Athabasca and Miette River Valleys, the town of Jasper and several mountain ranges. On a clear day the familiar, glaciated summit of Mt. Robson, 80 km to the northwest, is also visible. With an elevation of 3954 m/12,972 ft Robson is easily the highest mountain in the Canadian Rockies.

In the winter, skiing at Marmot Basin is among the best in the Rockies. Excellent cross-country skiing can be enjoyed almost anywhere around Jasper, most notably along a network of trails on the Pyramid Bench.

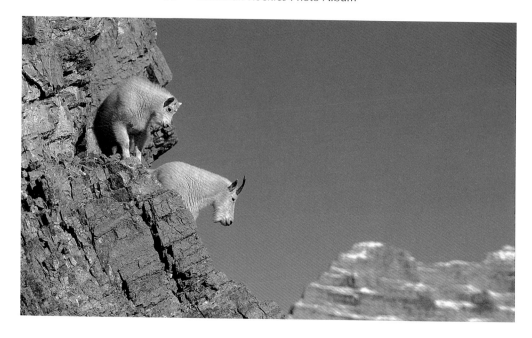

Mountain goats are most at home on a rocky cliff like this one, where grizzlies and other predators can't reach them.

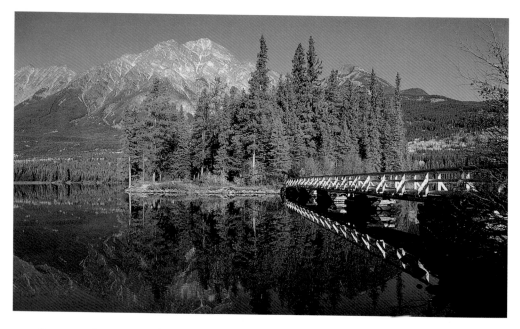

Pyramid is one of more than 40 lakes in the vicinity of Jasper townsite. Pyramid Mountain is seen in the distance.

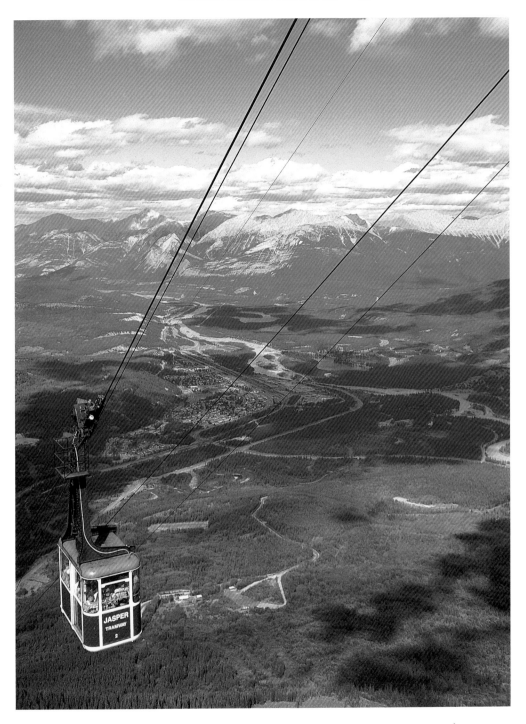

The Jasper Tramway climbs almost 1000 m (over 3000 ft) to the crest of Whistler Mountain, affording a breathtaking view of Mt. Robson, Maligne Lake and Jasper townsite.

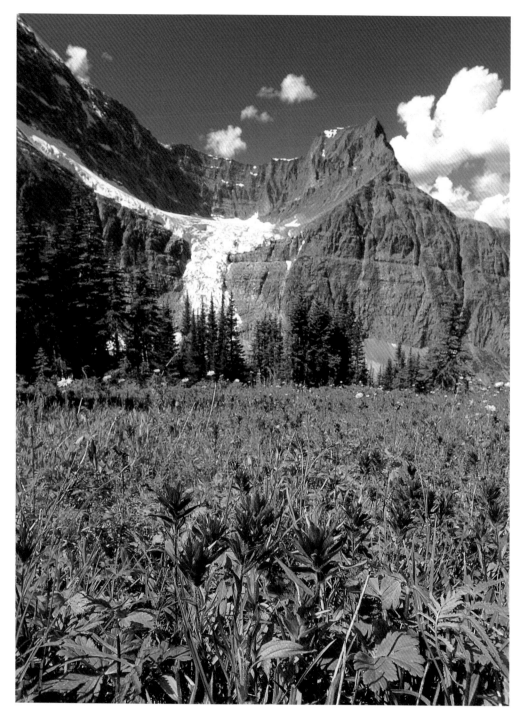

Angel Glacier on Mt. Edith Cavell, Jasper National Park.
The flowers in the foreground are called paintbrush.

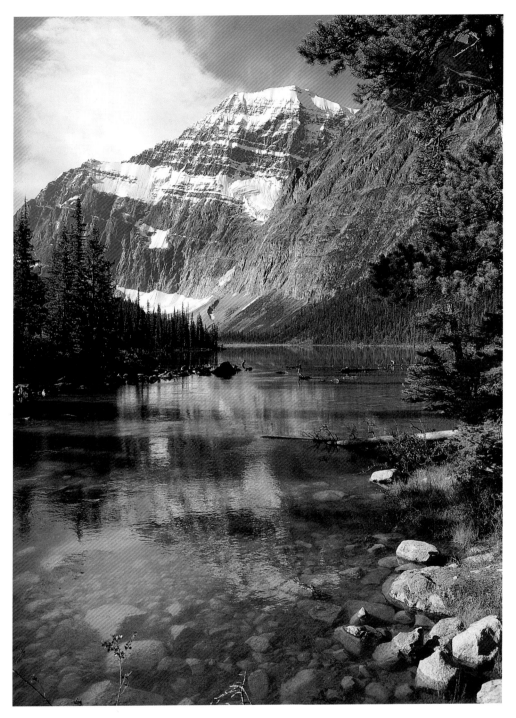

Mt. Edith Cavell was a much-used landmark in the days
of the fur trade, as its 3363 m/11,033 ft elevation makes it
one of the highest peaks near Jasper.

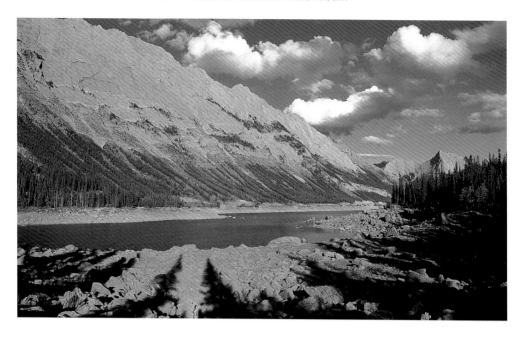

The waters of Jasper's Medicine Lake drain into a cave system
that empties into Maligne Canyon, 17 km downstream.

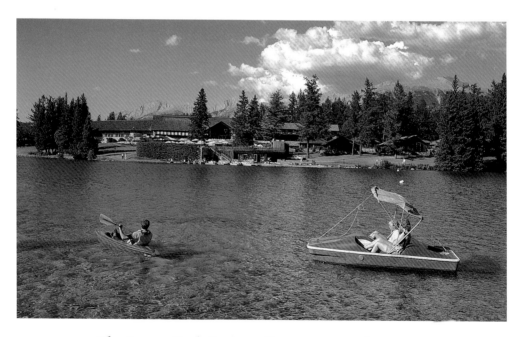

The Jasper Park Lodge offers accommodation
for 430 guests year-round.

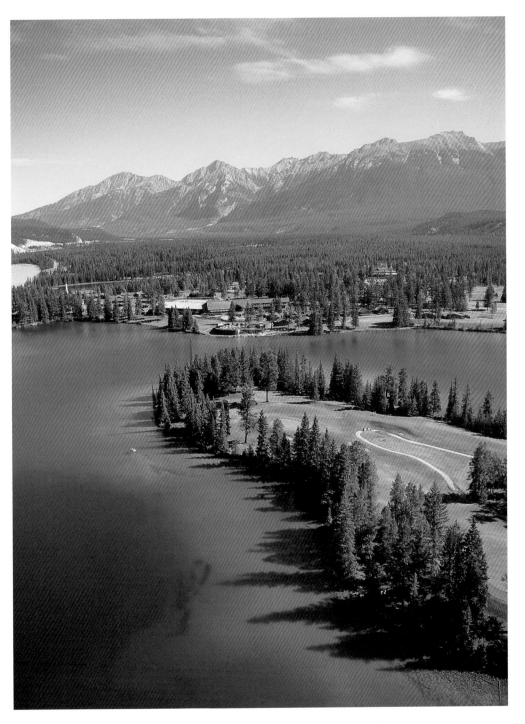

Aerial view of the Jasper Park Lodge,
Lac Beauvert and Old Man Mountain.

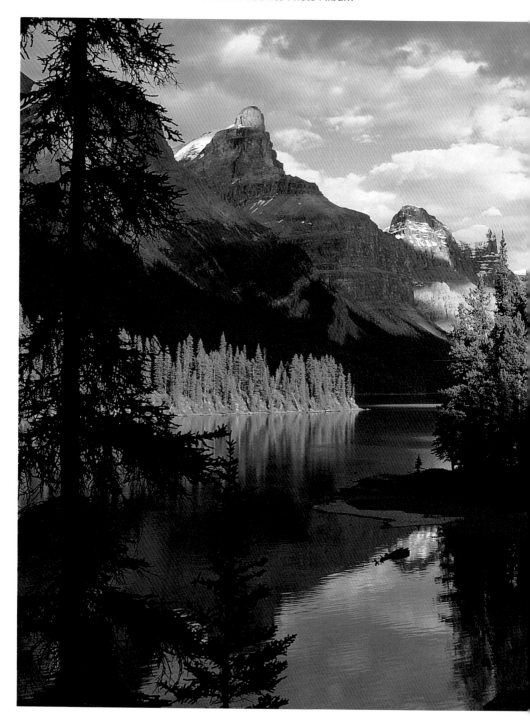

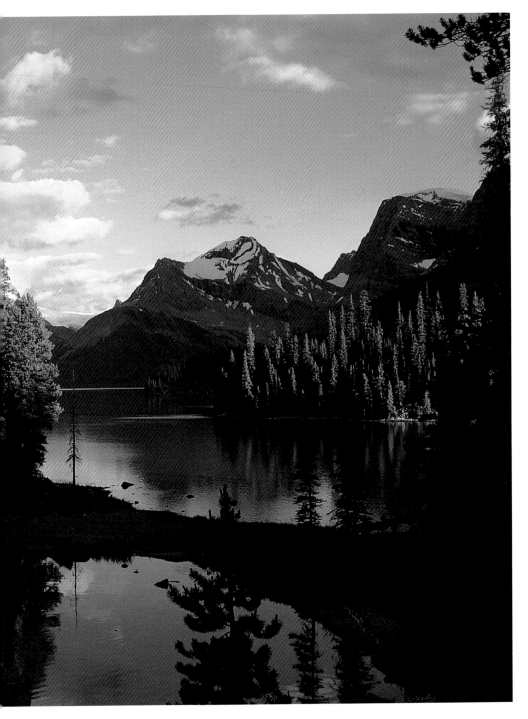

This spectacular view of Spirit Island has made Maligne Lake world-famous. Maligne is the largest lake in the Canadian Rockies.

The Maligne Lake Road

One of Jasper's treasures is the achingly beautiful view of Spirit Island on Maligne Lake, with glaciated peaks in the background. It is among the most photographed places in the Rockies, and for good reason. To fully appreciate the beauty of Maligne Lake, with its border of glaciers and high mountains, many visitors take a guided two-hour boat tour.

Maligne Canyon is the longest and deepest limestone canyon in the Canadian Rockies, and the view from any of the five bridges is dizzying – 50 m/165 ft straight down into the swirling, racing waters of the Maligne River, bound for its rendezvous with the Athabasca downstream.

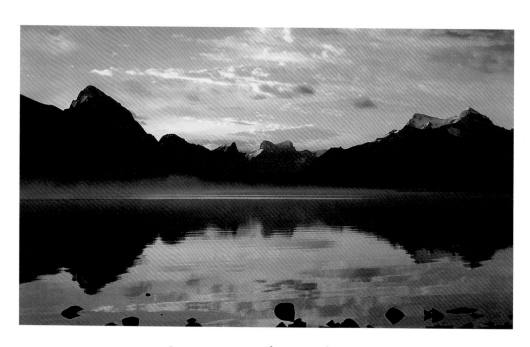

Sunrise on Maligne Lake.

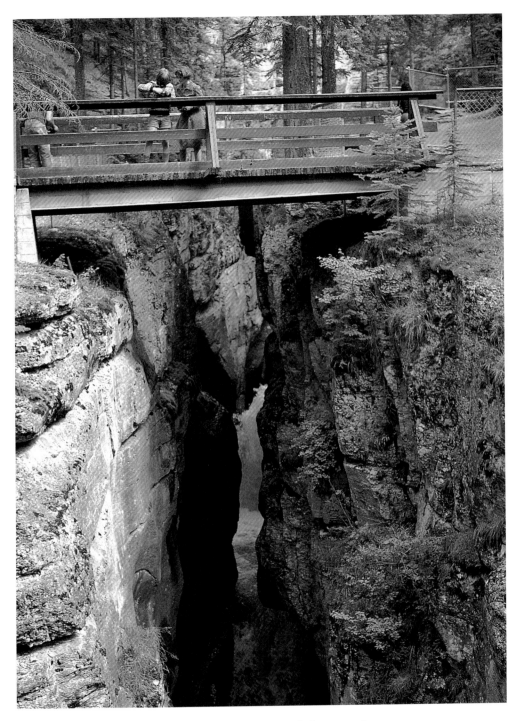

Maligne is the longest and deepest limestone
canyon in the Canadian Rockies.

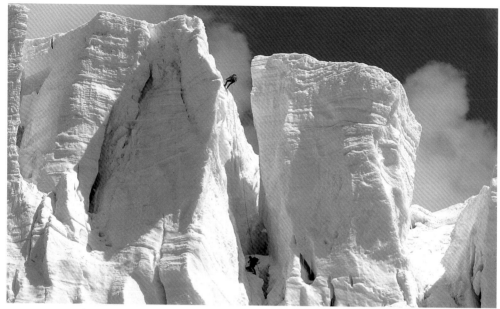

At 3954 m/12,972 ft, Mt. Robson is the highest peak in the Canadian Rockies. It is considered a choice mountaineering challenge.

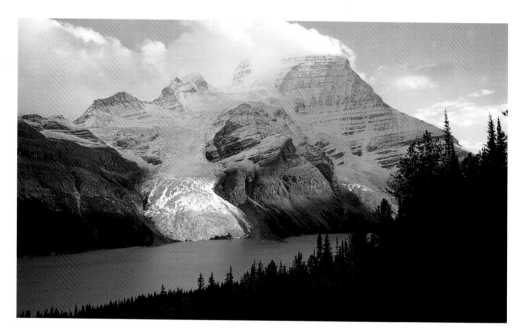

Because of its great height Robson creates its own weather, and the summit is often veiled in cloud. This makes climbing it – and photographing it – even more difficult.

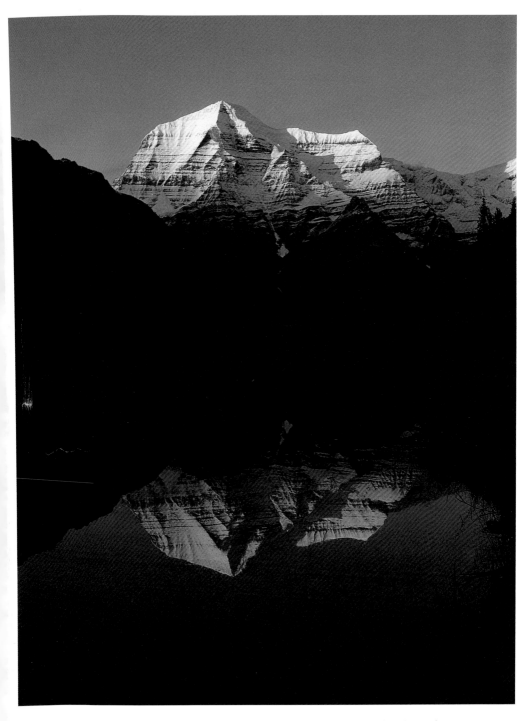

Alpenglow illuminates Mt. Robson for the last few
minutes of daylight on a summer evening.

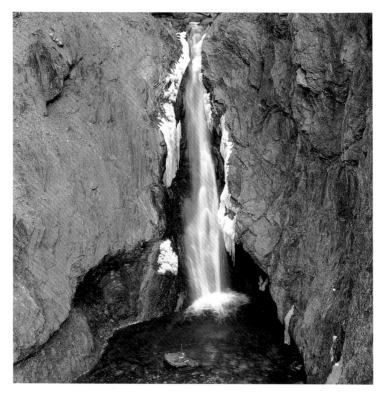

Waterfall near Wonder Pass,
Mt. Assiniboine Provincial Park.

Photo Credits

Van Christou: 9A, 9B, 54B, 66B, 78

Carole Harmon: 2, 5, 16B, 18A, 18B, 22A, 25B, 28A, 29, 30B,
31, 32A, 39, 42A, 42B, 43, 46A, 47, 50A, 56, 66A, 70B, 73A, 79B, 93

Don Harmon: FRONT COVER, 1, 11B, 12/13, 22B, 23, 24A, 36A,
36B, 38, 40A, 40B, 51, 52, 53, 60B, 62B, 64/65, 69, 77, 87, 96,
BACK COVER

Stephen Hutchings: 16A, 17, 21A, 27, 28B, 30A, 32B, 33, 46B,
48/49, 50B, 55, 57, 60A, 62A, 63, 68A, 68B, 73B, 76B, 79A, 80, 81,
84B, 85, 88A, 88B, 90/91, 92, 94B

Douglas Leighton: 24B

Harry Rowed: 95

Scott Rowed: 8, 11A, 19, 21B, 25A, 26, 37, 41, 54A, 61, 67,
70A, 71, 72, 74/75, 84A, 86, 89, 94A

R. W. Sandford: 76A